BREXIT
THE BENEFIT OF HINDSIGHT

Peace E. Ani is a financial services professional with over 15 years' industry experience. She has worked for leading global financial services institutions, across Investment Banking, Asset Management and the Specialty Insurance market. Peace completed her Brexit research as part of a post-graduate research project under the supervision of David Miles CBE, former member of the Monetary Policy Committee at the Bank of England. She published five op-ed articles on the impact of Brexit, based on her research.

Peace graduated with First class honours in Mathematical Sciences. She has an MBA from Imperial College Business School, and is also an Oxford University Scholar.

BREXIT:
THE BENEFIT OF HINDSIGHT

KING vs RICH TRADE-OFF

PEACE E. ANI

Matador
9 Priory Business Park,
Wistow Road, Kibworth Beauchamp,
Leicestershire. LE8 0RX
Tel: 0116 279 2299
Email: books@troubador.co.uk
Web: www.troubador.co.uk/matador
Twitter: @matadorbooks

ISBN 978 1838590 710

British Library Cataloguing in Publication Data.
A catalogue record for this book is available from the British Library.

Printed by CPI Group (UK) Ltd, Croydon, CR0 4YY
Typeset in 10.5pt Minion Pro by Troubador Publishing Ltd, Leicester, UK

Matador is an imprint of Troubador Publishing Ltd

To both the 'Leavers' and 'Remainers',
with the hope of better prospects for the future generation.

CONTENTS

QUOTATIONS FROM INTERVIEWS

The following quotations reflect a range of perspectives on the expected impact of Brexit:

"The standard of living in the UK may decline."

David Miles, CBE, Former member of the Monetary Policy Committee

(MPC)

"A real concern is that the next generation may not do as well as the current that have benefitted from the post-war advancement."

Dr Richard Ward, Former CEO, Lloyd's of London

"London's significance as a global financial centre may diminish, and shrinkage of the financial services industry is bad for the UK."

Nicola Horlick, CEO, Money & Co.

"Brexit may bring significant disruption and poses a risk of a potential UK break-up, further discouraging investors."

Jacob Nell, Chief UK Economist, Morgan Stanley

"Brexit presents a unique challenge."

Hayley Spink, Brexit Programme Director, Lloyd's of London

"Dublin may see a 5% growth, as it is perhaps the closest to the UK in terms of location, culture, language, and architecture."

Nicola Horlick, CEO, Money & Co.

ACKNOWLEDGEMENTS

The research for this book was completed as part of a postgraduate research project, and serves to add to the existing body of work with the objective of ensuring that the UK government, and UK-based businesses with an international footprint, are well positioned to benefit from any opportunities that may be a by-product of Brexit.

Although the author attempted to source data and reports from credible and reputable outlets, there is the acknowledgement that subjectivity might still exist in some reports and some commentary. This was mitigated through ensuring diverse media sources were utilised in order to improve the objectivity of the findings.

As the sand continues to shift under our feet, the Brexit process appears to unravel and reform at every turn. The full impact of Brexit is complex to analyse. What may be prescient conjecture one day is proven out of date the next, with many dynamics and disproportional impacts. It is likely to take several years before the full extent of the impact is known. Although all of the impact could not be addressed within the scope of this book, it is hoped that this adds to the existing body of work and provides a solid ground for future research.

I'm immensely grateful to Professor David Miles CBE, former member of the Monetary Policy Committee (MPC), for his supervision and guidance on the effective approach for the research.

A big thank you to all participants of the interviews, namely Nicola Horlick, a renowned businesswoman, entrepreneur and author; Dr Richard Ward, former CEO of Lloyd's of London insurance market and former CEO of International Petroleum Exchange (IPE); Jacob Nell, Chief UK Economist of Morgan Stanley; and Hayley Spink, Brexit Programme Director at Lloyd's of London, for sharing their opinions and expertise on the topic.

I owe particular thanks to my family and in-laws, my parents Mr and Mrs Peter Osalor for being role models with a strong work ethic. I'm especially grateful to my husband, CJ Ani, for his support, companionship and inspiration through everything. He has had to put up with endless discussions about Brexit and review several versions of this book. A special thank you to my uncle, Harold Johnson, for teaching me how to play chess (a strategy game) from an early age. Parallels have been drawn between the endgame manoeuvres in a chess game and the Brexit impasse. I have been fortunate to have Paul Roberts as the editor of this book. From his initial assessment and further feedback, I have been able to create a more polished output. I'm grateful to all of my friends, previous and current colleagues in the financial services industry, for their support, mentorship, and exposure. I'm grateful to Vlad Sarca, my executive class-mate at Oxford University who encouraged me to publish this book.

Above all, I am most thankful to God, the source of all my blessings.

NOTATIONS

Abbreviations	Definition
AG	Attorney General
AIFMD	Alternative Investment Fund Managers Directive
AUM	Assets Under Management
BBA	British Bankers' Association
BoE	Bank of England
CAD	Current Account Deficit
CBI	Confederation of Business Industry
CEP	Centre of Economic Performance
CETA	Comprehensive Economic and Trade Agreement
CPI	Consumer Prices Index
CRD IV	Capital Requirement Directive IV
DUP	Democratic Unionist Party
ECB	European Central Bank
ECSC	European Coal and Steel Community
EEA	European Economic Area
EEC	European Economic Community

EFTA	European Free Trade Agreement
EM	Emerging Market
EMIR	European Market Infrastructure Regulation
EU	European Union
FCA	Financial Conduct Authority
FDI	Foreign Direct Investment
FinTech	Financial Technology
GDP	Gross Domestic Product
GNP	Gross National Product
IDD	Insurance Distribution Directive
IFS	Institute for Fiscal Studies
IoD	Institute of Directors
IPE	International Petroleum Exchange
MiFID I & II	Markets in Financial Instruments Directive I & II
MPC	Monetary Policy Committee
NIESR	The National Institute of Economic and Social Research
NiGEM	National Institute Global Econometric Model
OECD	Organisation of Economic Co-operation and Development
ONS	Office of National Statistics
PSD II	Payment Services Directive II
QE	Quantitative Easing
SII	Solvency II
STEM	Science, Technology, Engineering and Mathematics
TFS	Term Funding Scheme
UCITS	Undertakings for Collective Investments in Transferable Securities
WTO	World Trade Organization
WWII	World War Two

INTRODUCTION

Brexit, a blend of 'British' and 'exit', is the term used to describe the decision of the United Kingdom (UK) to leave the European Union (EU). Some economists have described this decision as the UK taking a leap into the dark in an uncharted territory with dawn still quite far away. On the other hand, a 'Leaver' may describe it as a bright new dawn. Whilst Brexit is inherently political, this research focuses on the economic and financial markets consequences. A number of scenarios have been analysed as the basis to inform the findings and conclusions in this book.

The UK financial services industry produces annual revenues of approximately £200 billion, and contributes approximately £60–67 billion in taxes each year (according to a report by Oliver Wyman produced in 2016). The UK financial services industry combined with the related professional services sector are significant contributors to the UK economy, as they have evolved into an interdependent and interconnected ecosystem. Therefore, the effects of Brexit have a broader impact beyond the cross-border EU-related business, which is why the largest firms in the City have voiced strong support for continued access to the Single Market.

The UK is on the cusp of leaving the EU, and the prospect of leaving and the resulting uncertainty appear to have cost the UK economy. Although opportunities may arise from the uncertainty, the economic consequences of Brexit are dependent on the policies adopted by the UK. The findings suggest that Brexit may result in lower trade volumes for the UK due to reduced integration with the EU. An estimate of the cost of Brexit is 3% of GDP by 2020. Putting this into perspective, the cost of the 2008 global financial crisis to the UK was more than 10% of GDP according to a report from Chowla et al. from the Bank of England.

Although the decision to leave the EU following the referendum result has wide-scale implications for business across industries and has created some uncertainty, it also presents an opportunity for the UK to define new trading terms.

Upon leaving the EU, the UK will become a 'third country', which means that it will no longer be a member negotiating with the remaining EU27. In reality, this means that the UK becomes a rival to some extent, with implications of a potentially long trade agreement negotiation process. However, from an optimistic point of view, despite the complexity and inevitable longevity of the trade agreement process, the findings from the research suggest that it would increase most nations' collective prosperity to agree to a mutually beneficial trade deal with the UK.

The most recently completed trade agreement between the EU and Canada is the Comprehensive Economic and Trade Agreement (CETA). CETA sets a useful precedent for the UK to define its own unilateral trade agreement, perhaps called 'BRETA' – British Economic and Trade Agreement. Therefore, the UK is in a unique position to define its own unilateral agreement with the rest of the world.

Finally, it is worth noting that negotiating trade agreements is a long process and can take up to ten years to be agreed in some cases. Almost three years have already been spent negotiating the withdrawal agreement, yet still it has been rejected three times. The King vs. Rich concept which is discussed in detail in the final chapter, describes the trade-off decisions between wealth maximisation and control that entrepreneurs make as their empires grow. Those who don't figure out which is more important to them often end up neither wealthy nor powerful. This framework has been used as the basis to answer the question - what does the UK want?.

CHAPTER 1

How We Got Here: 52%/48%

British exit from the European Union (EU), commonly known as Brexit, is the ending of the UK's membership of the EU. The result of the referendum held on 23 June 2016 on the UK's EU membership was a majority of 51.9% voting to leave, with 48.1% voting to remain. The UK Prime Minister initiated the formal withdrawal procedure, known as triggering Article 50, on 29 March 2017. According to Ivan Rogers, the UK's former ambassador to the EU, in his essays *9 Lessons in Brexit*, this was not a strong opening move, early on the UK needed to 'recognise the complexity and inevitable longevity of the exit process, work out the viable options with clarity about what the UK wants in terms of what Brexit means – working through the very tough choices on the table'.

This book is primarily focused on one aspect of the Brexit debate, which is the impact on the UK's financial services industry (the City) – deemed one of the most vulnerable to the negative outcomes of Brexit – and the knock-on effect of this on the rest of the UK economy. While the City overwhelmingly voted for the UK's continued membership of the EU, a significant portion of financial services employers voted to leave, and through my research from the interview discussions, their rationale didn't appear to be driven by anti-immigration or xenophobic sentiments, but rather a rational assessment of the cost and benefit of the EU membership.

The global financial crisis of 2008 led to mounting public anger and hostility towards the financial services sector in the wake of the bank bail-outs. Despite the deep-rooted fault lines between the sector and the rest of the UK, which 'Brexit has graphically exposed', the City is an important sector according to the blog by Warren et al (2019). Although, it is by no means the only sector that matters, where possible, the various economic indicators and the broader impact of Brexit will be discussed.

Before exploring the UK's options (most of which have been rejected by MPs at the time of writing), and what the UK wants now, let me first provide some context about why the UK joined the EU in the first place.

The Background to the EU Referendum

WHAT IS THE EU?

The EU, a political and economic union, consists of twenty-eight member states located in Europe, with an estimated population of over 500 million (European Union, 2016). The European Single Market was developed by the EU through a standardised system of laws and policies. These policies ensure free movement of people, services, and money within this Single Market, through maintaining common policies on trade and regional development.

Representing approximately 6.9% of the world's population, in 2016 the EU generated a nominal GDP of $16.5 trillion. This represents approximately 22.2% of global nominal GDP but 16.9% in purchasing power parity terms (European Union, 2016).

The EU consists of the following seven principal decision-making bodies that operate through a supranational and intergovernmental hybrid system.

Table 1: EU Decision-Making Bodies

EU decision-making bodies	i. European Council
	ii. Council of the European Union
	iii. European Parliament
	iv. European Commission
	v. Court of Justice of the European Union
	vi. European Central Bank
	vii. European Court of Auditors

As a result of this global influence, the EU has been described as a superpower (Hill, 2016). Figure 1 illustrates the structural development and integration of the union since 1948, driven by international treaties.

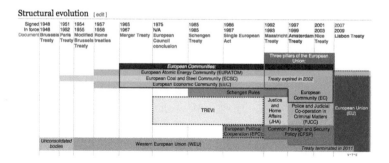

Figure 1: EU structural evolution
Source: EU, Wikipedia

GOVERNANCE

The EU has seven institutions, as set out previously, and the European Central Bank (ECB) determines the monetary policy of the Eurozone. The Court of Justice is responsible for the interpretation and the application of EU law and the European Court of Auditors examines the EU budget (European Union, 2016).

THE EU REFERENDUM RESULTS: INITIAL IMPACT

In the wake of the UK referendum results, where the UK voted to leave the EU, some described feeling a sense of mourning, but no one could immediately tangibly articulate what had been lost. At the same time, some felt that the best outcome for the country had been achieved, with some politico-religious bloggers describing the unexpected result indicative of it being 'an act of God'. This is interesting food for thought, as in the insurance sector, an 'act of God' colloquially refers to any event that occurs outside of human control and that can't be predicted or prevented. Severe weather - hurricanes, earthquakes, floods and storms - are all considered acts of God. Insurance policies often contain an act of God clause, which is designed to protect insurers from hefty pay-outs associated with such unpredictable events. Although the markets initially responded quite negatively, with the British Pound exchange rate falling to a thirty-year low against the US Dollar, the markets recovered quickly. However, it was suggested that it was possible that the results of the US election in November 2016 may have positively impacted the sterling exchange rate. The Brexit result seemed to have temporarily destabilised the status quo, but without changing anything, although the uncertainty initially appeared to have been costly to the economy as illustrated in Figure 2 .

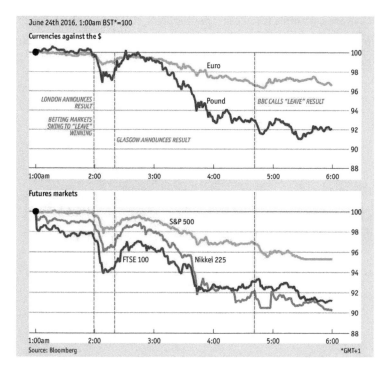

Figure 2: The initial market reaction to the EU referendum results

Source: Bloomberg, The Economist

However, within a few weeks, per Figure 3, the markets had rapidly recovered and the FTSE 100 is, at the time of writing, higher than before the referendum.

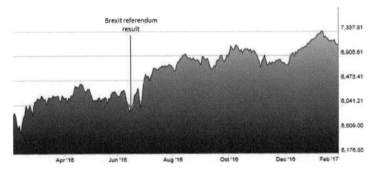

Figure 3: FTSE 100 index following the referendum result

Source: Bloomberg

WHY DID THE UK JOIN THE EU IN THE FIRST PLACE?

In the financial services community the Brexit result created a lot of uncertainty and concerns about another potential global financial crisis. The global financial crisis, which occurred in 2008, grabbed the attention of society, and eight years later, the belief that Brexit is perhaps an aftershock of the 2008 crisis may not seem so far-fetched. Whilst it could be argued that the financial crisis was bound to happen sometime, likened to 'catching a falling knife' whenever it happened, it still would have been painful. Perhaps the same rationale could be applied here, as it seems the UK was usually the unwilling partner in the relationship. The UK is 'divorcing' the EU after forty-five years. Whilst it wasn't necessarily a marriage made in heaven from a financial services perspective, it is not clear whether the UK will be better off outside the marriage. As food for thought, staying with the marriage and divorce analogy, could the marriage between the EU and UK still be saved through counselling (renegotiation) by working through and resolving the points that are causing friction in the marriage, or is it the case that the marriage has completely broken down with 'irreconcilable differences'? I share this consideration, because following the referendum result and protracted withdrawal agreement negotiations, the realities of a hard Brexit have huge economic, social, political and legal consequences. Through the rest of the book, I will explore the trade-offs between sovereignty, national control and access to the Single Market, the latter being described by Ivan Rogers (the UK's former ambassador to the EU) as 'our biggest market for our goods and services'.

First, an analysis of the UK economy since 1945 provides a useful context as to why the UK joined the EU in the first place, and allows for a complete assessment of the motive and potential impact of Brexit.

THE UK ECONOMY SINCE 1945

Christopher Gandrud (lecturer of International Politics at City University London) analyses how the UK economy was impacted after joining the EU. Between most of 1945–1973, the UK economy was often described as the 'sick man of Europe', due to its relatively weak economic performance compared to other European countries.

This narrative started to change from 1973 upon joining the European Economic Community (EEC), an early version of what is now known as the EU (Gandrud, 2016). The EEC progressively sought investor-friendly and pro-market policies, such as the Single European Act of 1986, leading to the formation of the Single Market. Permitting free trade and labour movement led to increased returns from investing in the UK.

However, whilst some of the increase in investments in the 1980s could be attributable to the EEC membership, there were a number of initiatives by the ruling government at the time from the late 1970s, such as trade union legislations, which may also have played a significant role. A number of international companies increased their investment in the UK to enable access to the Single

Market. The increased investment during this period seemed common across the large EU economies, as seen in Figure 4.

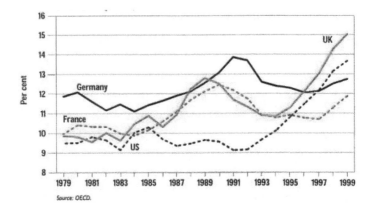

Figure 4: Business investment as a share of GDP, 1979–1999 (constant prices)

Whilst the narrow Brexit vote may not return the UK to a similar weak economic environment of pre-1973, the key to a successful Brexit negotiation will be to agree a deal that will maintain the current level of prosperity, as well as achieving the several other objectives inferred in the referendum question (e.g. a reduction in net immigration).

See Insert A for the timeline of events leading to the EU referendum.

TIMELINE OF EVENTS

The timeline provides the history and context of the UK's entry into the EU, whilst at the same time suggesting the cultural influences which have shaped Britain's relationship with Europe, including Charles de Gaulle's initial refusal to let Britain enter.

In the next chapter I analyse how the referendum result has led to increased uncertainty.

Insert A – timeline of events leading to the EU referendum

1957-1974	1975-1983	1984-1992	1993-2012	2013-2015	2016
1957: Treaty of Rome created the EEC. 1963-67: UK applied to join the organisation in 1963 and again in 1967, but both applications were vetoed. On 1 January 1973, the UK joined the EEC, or 'Common Market'. The opposition Labour Party, led by Harold Wilson, contested the October 1974 general election with a commitment to renegotiate Britain's terms of membership of the EEC and then hold a referendum on whether to remain in the EEC on the new terms.	In 1975, the UK held a referendum on whether to remain in the EEC. All of the major political parties and mainstream press supported continuing membership of the EEC. In 1979, the UK opted out of the newly formed European Exchange Rate Mechanism (ERM) which was the precursor to the creation of the euro. 1983: The opposition Labour Party campaigned in the 1983 general election on a commitment to withdraw from the EEC without a referendum. It was heavily defeated as the Conservative government of Margaret Thatcher was re-elected.	In October 1990, despite the deep reservations of Prime Minister Margaret Thatcher but under pressure from her senior ministers, the UK joined the ERM. In September 1992, the UK was forced to withdraw from the ERM after the pound sterling came under pressure from currency speculators (an episode known as Black Wednesday). The resulting cost to UK taxpayers was estimated to be in excess of £3 billion.	As a result of the Maastricht Treaty, the EEC became the European Union on 1 November 1993. The new name reflected the evolution of the organisation from an economic union to a political union. The UK Independence Party (UKIP), a Eurosceptic political party, was also formed, in 1993. In 2012, Prime Minister David Cameron rejected calls for a referendum on the UK's EU membership, but suggested the possibility of a future referendum to gauge public support. According to the BBC, "The prime minister acknowledged the need to ensure the UK's position within the European Union had 'the full-hearted support of the British people' but they needed to show 'tactical and strategic patience.'"	Under pressure from many of his MPs and from the rise of UKIP, in January 2013, Cameron announced that a Conservative government would hold an in-out referendum on EU membership before the end of 2017 on a renegotiated package, if elected in 2015. The European Referendum Act 2015 was introduced into Parliament to enable the referendum. Despite being in favour of remaining in a reformed European Union himself, Cameron announced that Conservative Ministers and MPs were free to campaign in favour of remaining in the EU or leaving it.	On 22 February 2016, Cameron announced a referendum date of 23 June 2016 and set out the legal framework for the withdrawal from the European Union in circumstances where there was a referendum majority vote to leave, citing Article 50 of the Lisbon Treaty. The result was announced on the morning of 24 June: 51.9% voted in favour of leaving the European Union and 48.1% voted in favour of remaining a member of the EU. David Cameron stood down on 13 July, with Theresa May becoming Prime Minister. In October 2016, Theresa May announced the March 2017 deadline for triggering Article 50, and also promised a 'Great Repeal Bill', which would repeal the European Communities Act 1972 and restate in UK law all enactments previously in force under EU law.

CHAPTER 2

Uncertainty

Future historians may not be short of material for 2019, not least because of the goings-on in Prime Minister Theresa May's government and the resignations of high profile ministers and her Brexit Secretaries. They may, in hindsight, find the sequence of events, the negotiations with the EU, and the rounds of presentation and rejection of Mrs May's deal, humorous, notwithstanding the magnitude of the process and future prosperity of the country at stake. Whilst all of this may provide good anecdotes for heated debates, for business, the key priority is certainty.

Whatever the outcome of Brexit, these are not 'normal' times. Businesses and trade leaders have been preparing for Brexit and its impact on business operations by executing their contingency plans. This is discussed further in Chapter 4 under the no-deal Brexit scenario. It appears that only businesses that are up to date, nimble with their finger on the pulse, and well connected will thrive, by turning the uncertainty into opportunities.

However, before I discuss what these future opportunities may entail, it is worth analysing what opportunities joining the EU created for the UK back in 1973.

Changes to the UK's Living Standards Following EU Membership

Much of the economic evidence sourced from the Organisation for Economic Co-operation and Development (OECD) suggests that remaining in the EU may be better than leaving. For example, since joining the EU in 1973, UK GDP per capita has increased more than other comparable countries outside the EU over the same period: see Figure 5.

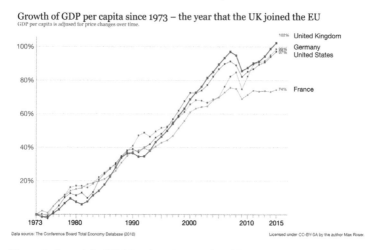

Growth of GDP per capita since 1973 – the year that the UK joined the EU
GDP per capita is adjusted for price changes over time.

Data source: The Conference Board Total Economy Database (2016)
Licensed under CC-BY-SA by the author Max Roser.

Figure 5: Growth in UK GDP since EU membership

Additionally, numerous pieces of evidence suggest that the UK and the EU are both economically stronger with the UK as a member: see Figure 6. The EU's share of the world's total GDP and trade are smaller when the UK's contribution is excluded. Therefore, Brexit may negatively impact the EU's leading GDP position when the UK leaves the EU, placing the EU behind the US and China. This perhaps explains why the EU is reluctant to let the UK leave.

On the other hand, there is some evidence suggesting that changes in domestic policies partly explain the UK's strong performance. The

'Big Bang' occurred in the 1980s. According to economists Nick Crafts, restrictive banking policies encouraged businesses to look for opportunities outside of the United States.

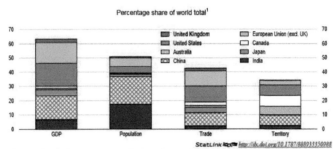

Percentage share of world total[1]

StatLink http://dx.doi.org/10.1787/888933350088

1. Data for GDP adjusted for purchasing power parity (PPP) refer to 2014. Data for population refer to 2013. Population figures for Canada and the European Union refers to 2012. Data for trade (i.e. sum of exports and imports of goods and services) refer to 2014. Trade data for the United Kingdom and the European Union exclude intra-EU trade. Data for territory refer to 2015.

Source: IMF (2015), *World Economic Outlook Database*, October 2015, International Monetary Fund; OECD (2016), *OECD Population Statistics* (database), April; and World Bank (2016), *World Development Indicators* (database), April.

Figure 6: Global economic power of the UK relative to the EU

Therefore, with the impending exit, this may present new opportunities for the UK as a global leading financial hub, along with the expected challenges. Hence, it is economically important for the UK to agree a deal that retains as much access as possible to the Single Market, but with improved control of borders in order to assuage the electorate.

See Insert B for the perceived winners and losers of the Brexit outcome.

The Cost of Uncertainty

Almost three years since the referendum, the UK's corporate sector is still gripped by the uncertainty of Brexit. Although macroeconomic data from the Office of National Statistics (ONS) shows a limited impact of Brexit on household spending, there are pockets of the economy where the Brexit uncertainty impact is felt. The housing market and the car and furniture industries have experienced some decline as reported by Korczak et al., where their 'results suggest that the market expects a longer-term negative impact of Brexit on consumer spending, which is likely to result when relocations and reductions in corporate investment start impacting local job markets and disposable income'.

The precise effect of Brexit is uncertain, as are the potential agreements to be reached on trade and immigration policy, all of which contribute to uncertainties about the UK's growth prospects. According to economist Jacob Nell, the increase in uncertainty may lead to a reduction in consumption and investment, Foreign Direct Investment (FDI), and the resulting effect on GDP could have a longer-term negative effect on productivity. This view was also shared by Mark Carney in a speech at the Bank of England (BoE) in London in 2016:

> "All this uncertainty has contributed to a form of economic post-traumatic stress disorder among households and businesses, as well as in financial markets, leading to some deterioration in the economic outlook."

In hindsight, and as illustrated in Figure 3 in the previous chapter, this has not necessarily squared up with the relatively positive performance of the economy. However, according to Korczak et al. of the University of Bristol Business department, investment fell for four consecutive quarters in 2018, the first time since the financial crisis (as reported by the Office for National Statistics). Additionally, a survey by the Confederation of British Industry indicated that 80% of businesses considered Brexit uncertainty to have had a negative impact on their investment decisions. Whilst the economy as a whole seems relatively stable at the time of writing, the reduced business investment will have a negative impact on the long-term growth prospects of UK firms as we approach the end of the withdrawal period and contend with the prospect of actually leaving the EU.

"The UK could possibly move from being the fifth to the seventh biggest economy in the world, therefore setting the UK economy backwards."

Nicola Horlick, CEO, Money & Co.

Some of the short- and long-run drivers of uncertainty identified through the interviews are illustrated in Figure 7.

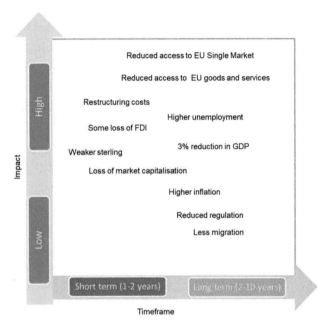

Figure 7: The drivers of uncertainty for the Financial Services industry

See Insert C for specific economic features of the Brexit debate and whether they are expected to be negatively or positively impacted.

Within the financial services industry, contingency plans have been executed, such as relocating staff, operations and assets. According to a survey by EY published in January 2019, 36% of financial services firms and 56% of banks and brokerage firms have relocated staff and operations overseas as a result of Brexit. This is consistent with an article titled 'Brexodus: why fund firms are moving billions of pounds out of UK', where several large asset managers have moved money out of the UK as more fund groups start making their Brexit contingency plans. 'Uncertainty' over Brexit negotiations has been identified as the main reason for the switch.

However, it's not all doom and gloom; in the same article cited, there are a number of large US firms who still find the UK attractive and are looking at setting up UK funds, namely Open Ended Investment Company (OEICs) ranges. These will mirror their Société d'Investissement à Capital Variable (SICAV) funds, (meaning 'investment company with variable capital'), a publicly traded open-ended investment fund structure offered in Europe.

This means that it is a company that exists to invest in the shares of other companies (investment company) and that it can create or cancel new shares according to investor demand (variable capital). OEICs are professionally managed collective investment funds. A fund manager pools money from many investors and buys shares, bonds, property, or cash assets and other investments.

In the next section, we explore what opportunities could be exploited in the midst of the chaos and uncertainty.

The Opportunities of Uncertainty

Historically, challenges and uncertainties in the economy also present opportunities. The key is to identify where the opportunities are, and then take a strategic and sometimes innovative approach to exploring those opportunities. Businesses are in a unique position, as the referendum result means the UK now has the opportunity to define new trading agreements with its trading partners, and maximise the opportunities that a new trading model will present whilst minimising any negative impacts on their business model and the UK economy.

According to a report by the Confederation of Business Industry (CBI), 20% of businesses have found some opportunities for business growth that may arise out of Brexit. Of those, 33% of businesses identified disruption to existing markets as providing an opportunity in relation to Brexit.

Although the EU and its member states remain the primary market for the UK's financial services products (representing approximately a third of the total exported, according to a report by the City of London Corporation), the UK has developed strong and growing trade relationships with several countries outside of the EU. Furthermore, the 'strength of the financial services cluster in London, and the wealth and availability of skilled professionals, legal, and technology services all underpin the capital's reputation as a world leading financial centre. With these strengths, there is good reason to believe that the UK's financial services industry can continue to prosper outside of the EU', according to the City of London Corporation .

Additionally, the City of London Corporation (and in particular, the Economic Development Office) has stated that they 'will be significantly increasing their investment to support financial services across the UK, reinforcing our strategy and delivery in building future products and services in financial services, promoting exports and investment, strengthening and influencing the wider regulatory framework, and enhancing our partnerships with business and government'.

Many institutions' priority is to ensure minimal disruption to their business and their ability to service clients. However, a key issue for financial institutions appears to be the outcome on 'passporting' and maintaining access to the Single Market. Passporting is the right for EU members to offer financial services across the European Economic Area (EEA) without further authorisation in each country, thereby leading to significant cost savings.

The financial services ecosystem dynamic suggests that additional activities may leave the UK if economies of scale are lost, thereby extending beyond EU-related activities, and negatively impacting UK GDP.

A 3% reduction in GDP by 2020 is the OECD's estimate of the economic cost of Brexit. To put this in context, according to economist David Miles, the average annual rate of growth has been 2% in the last 100 years. By 2020, a 3% reduction in GDP equates to being about eighteen months behind in growth terms. The global financial crisis of 2008 led to GDP being over 10% lower as illustrated in Figure 8.

Therefore in relative terms, although not insignificant, 3% is not a disaster, according to economist David Miles.

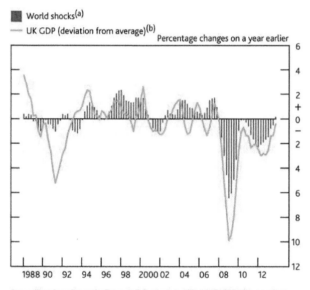

Source: Bloomberg, Bureau for Economic Policy Analysis, IMF, OECD, ONS, Thomson Reuters DataStream and Bank calculations

Figure 8: Estimates of the impact of world shocks on UK GDP

In the following chapter, I cover the financial services industry's contribution to the UK economy and the expected short- and long-term impact of Brexit on the sector and the UK economy.

CHAPTER 3

Brexit, Financial Services, and the UK Economy

According to the report by Oliver Wyman produced in 2016, the financial services industry produces annual revenues of approximately £200 billion and is therefore a significant contributor to the economy, contributing approximately £60–67 billion in taxes annually. The financial services industry also contributes a trade surplus of approximately £58 billion to the UK balance of payments annually according to the report by Sants et al. (2016). Therefore, the effects of Brexit may be felt more broadly than in the direct EU business transactions.

Much of the evidence suggests that the UK's financial services industry's prosperity is attributable to European integration and the Single Market. Therefore, the realities of Brexit could lead to significant shrinkage in this industry. Some commentators such as Nicolas Véron (a senior fellow at Bruegel and at the Peterson Institute for International Economics in Washington in DC) believe that this may lead to a negative impact on the national economy, not just the City.

"The jewel in the crown for London is the insurance sector, due to the high concentration of talent."

Dr Richard Ward, Former CEO, Lloyd's of London

As a leading financial centre, the UK has a significant proportion of business (22%) generated from EU-related activities, as illustrated in Figure 9, such as euro-denominated derivatives clearing.

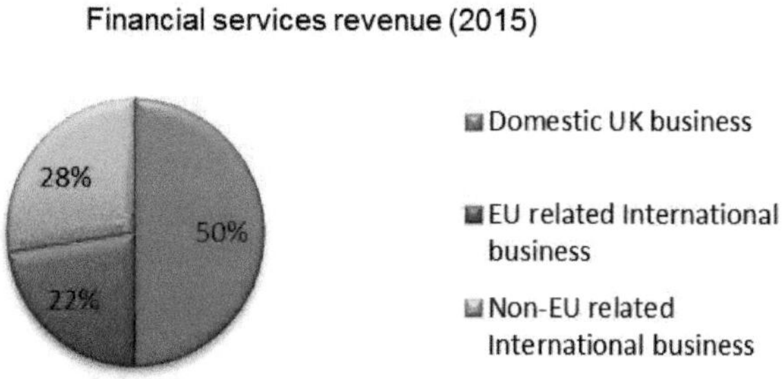

Financial services revenue (2015)

- Domestic UK business
- EU related International business
- Non-EU related International business

Figure 9: Breakdown of sources of financial services revenue

In order to estimate the potential impact of Brexit on the UK's financial services industry and GDP, the range of services and clients are important considerations.

Financial services sector activities

Investment Banking	Specialist Insurance	Investment management	Other related services
Sales and trading	Corporate clients' complex risks	Hedge funds Pension funds	Data services IT services
Hedging interest rates and FX exposures			
Raising capital			
International currency trades			

Figure 10: Financial services sector activities

The services as illustrated in Figure 10 include providing specialty insurance for complex risks, trading bonds and equities, hedging interest rate and foreign currency exposures, asset management, providing data and technology services to businesses and consumers, capital raising, and clearing and providing the market infrastructure (Sants et al., 2016).

Table 2 provides a more granular sectoral breakdown of the labour force and annual revenues produced by the financial services industry.

TABLE 2: QUANTIFICATION OF THE FINANCIAL SERVICES INDUSTRY IN THE UK

Although the financial services industry came under a lot of scrutiny following the global financial crisis of 2008, the industry's contribution to the UK economy in terms of GDP and employment is significant. Furthermore, the UK is regarded as one of the leading financial centres. As can be seen at the far bottom right of the table, this industry employs over a million people combined, their annual tax contribution is between £60–67 billion.

THE FINANCIAL SERVICES ECOSYSTEM

According to the same report by Sants et al. of Oliver Wyman, the financial services industry operates in an ecosystem comprising various financial and related professional services firms. The degree of interdependency within the financial services ecosystem means that the impact of Brexit may extend beyond business transacted directly with EU clients. For example, if a firm loses access to serve EU clients it may also lose the scale to operate profitably in the UK, and may therefore exit completely. Additionally, an activity operating adjacent to another related activity may relocate if the activity on which it co-depends were to leave the UK.

Table 2: Quantification of the Financial Services industry in the UK

Sectors	Annual Revenues (£Bn)/ Volume (where relevant)	Annual GVA (£Bn)	Annual Tax (£Bn)	Employment ('000)
Sales and Trading	~30	13-16	7-9	55-65
Investment Banking	10-12	5-7	3-4	~15
Retail and Business Banking	58-67	35-39	17-19	450-470
Private Banking and Wealth Management	5-6	3-4	1-2	21-26
Banking	108-117	55-61	29-33	540-565
Asset Management (REV/AUM)	20-23/~7Tn	14-18	5-7	40-50
Domestic Retail and Commercial (GDP/GWP)	27-29/150-155	21-23	9-10	260-290
Corporate and Specialty (GDP/GWP)	8-10/50-53	7-9	3-4	43-46
Reinsurance (GDP/GWP)	2-4/16-18	2-3	1-2	~5
Insurance and Reinsurance (GDP/GWP)	39-42/215-225	30-33	13-15	310-335
Exchanges, Clearing & Inter-Dealer Broking	3-4	2-3	1-3	10-12
Securities Services	3-4	2-3	~1	30-40
Technology, Data and Other	16-20	13-15	6-8	80-90
Marketing Infrastructure & Other	22-26	16-20	9-11	120-140
Total Financial Services	190-205	120-125	60-67	~1050

Sources: Oliver Wyman

Table 3: The benefits of this ecosystem

Benefits	Description
Enhanced service value chain	Enhanced service provision within the value chain as a result of the proximity and mutual understanding;
Innovation	Innovation driven by talent concentration and competition;
Economies of scale	Economies of scale in operational costs and financial resources;
Centres of excellence	Centres of excellence such as specialty insurance, and a variety of specialist professional services firms working interdependently within the sector; and
Regulatory framework	An effective regulatory framework for an efficient and innovative financial services.

Source: adapted by author from Oliver Wyman research

THE SHORT-TERM IMPLICATIONS

The initial impact of the referendum results appears to be weaker sterling, a rise in inflation, and an increased cost of borrowing. The Oliver Wyman report by Sants et al. (2016), produced for CityUK, and titled *The impact of the UK's exit from the EU on the UK-based financial services sector*, provides a more detailed analysis of the short-run implications on the UK financial services.

> "Brexit is using up a lot of senior management oxygen."
>
> Jacob Nell, Chief UK Economist, Morgan Stanley

Data from the FCA published in September 2016 indicated that approximately 5,500 UK firms relied on 'passporting' to conduct EU-wide business (Treanor, 2016).

"Passporting is a very efficient way for our customers to access Lloyd's specialist underwriting expertise. The passporting regime results in minimal reporting and no additional capital requirements under a single regulator."

Hayley Spink, Brexit Programme Director, Lloyd's of London

Assuming that the UK ends up with reduced access to the Single Market, the impact across the various financial services sectors based on the quantum of EU-related business that may be lost is summarised in Table 4 as follows:

Table 4: The impact of reduced access to the Single Market

Specialty insurance	Lloyd's and its ninety-seven syndicates are potentially impacted.
	Lloyd's contributes 20% of the UK financial services' GDP, employing 48,000 people (Beale, 2016).
Investment banking	UK firms would be prohibited from selling products directly to EU clients, although EU entities could transfer securities to a UK entity for risk management purposes (Sants et al., 2016).
Asset management	UK-based asset management firms would be prohibited from distributing to EU clients directly, but portfolio management could still be delegated to the UK (Sants et al., 2016).

Source: adapted by author from various sources

An article by Kollewe (2016) provides useful insight into how the specialty insurance sector may be impacted by Brexit: 'Unless agreements were reached with individual member states, UK specialty insurers and brokers would not be able to service EU clients.'

The entire value chain, including portfolio management, risk management, underwriters and brokers, may need to move to an EU entity. According to Kollewe, some leaders in the Specialty Insurance sector, including Lloyd's CEO, are considering cities such as Dublin,

Brussels and Frankfurt. This is a key consideration for Lloyd's as the business could lose up to £800 million of premiums from loss of passporting rights, representing 4% of the business. However, nearly £3 billion could be at risk, as 11% of Lloyd's of London's premiums comes from continental Europe (Kollewe 2016).

> *"In the short run the UK economy may be negatively impacted by losing consumers who are big spenders and contributors to the economy."*
>
> Nicola Horlick, CEO, Money & Co

THE LONG-TERM IMPLICATIONS
It has been estimated that by 2030 GDP may be between 1.5% and 3.7% lower than if the UK had remained in the EU. Real wages are forecast to fall by between 2.2% and 6.3%, and consumption to fall by between 2.4% and 5.4% (Ebell & Warren, 2016). Real wages and consumption may decline more than GDP in the long term as a result of trade deterioration and a shift towards savings. However, if interest rates became negative this could lead to more consumption (Ebell & Warren, 2016).

> *"Brexit was not about economic benefits."*
>
> Dr Richard Ward, Former CEO, Lloyd's of London

The economic indicators are further discussed in order to estimate the impact of Brexit on the UK economy.

UK GDP GROWTH
According to economist David Miles CBE, economic growth, measured by the change in GDP, is based on the value of goods and services produced in a given period. Most estimates suggest that GDP would be negatively impacted and could be materially lower in the long run when the UK leaves the EU. A lower GDP will result in lower public spending.

However, there are significant variations in the negative effects scale, driven by the following considerations:

i.   A number of the models suggest that the cost of Brexit will be lower if the UK can replicate the current access to the Single Market through European Economic Area (EEA) membership. Contrastingly, the cost may be greater if the UK moves from the current model and becomes reliant on World Trade Organization (WTO) rules (Emmerson et al., 2016).

ii. The dynamic effects of trades, which take into account the knock-on effects of reduced trade on productivity across the economy. According to the studies by National Institute of Economic and Social Research (NIESR), Centre for Economic Performance (CEP), and HM Treasury, these dynamic effects could lead to GDP being 7% lower in the long run (by 2030) than it would have been otherwise, compared to the baseline forecast in which the UK remains in the EU.

An impartial assumption for public finances suggests that spending and tax will remain proportionate to GDP. Therefore, a lower GDP will result in lower public spending. Based on NIESR's most pessimistic scenario, this may lead to public spending being £48 billion lower in 2030, or £7 billion lower in the more optimistic cases.

The UK's notional gross contribution to the EU in 2014 was £18.8 billion (HM Treasury, 2016), which represents 1% of GDP, and is equivalent to £350 million on a weekly basis, the widely reported figure. However, a more accurate figure is £14.4 billion, which takes into account the rebate paid by the EU (equivalent to £275 million per week). The EU returns a significant fraction of this £14.4 billion, although the amount varies – on average the UK's net contribution is £8 billion a year (Emmerson et al., 2016).

Although it initially appears that leaving the EU may improve the UK's public finances by £8 billion, assuming that the UK doesn't agree to an alternative deal that involves contributions to the EU budget, the consensus from various studies is that the net impact may be negative both in the short and long run due to increased uncertainty, leading to higher costs of trade and possibly reduced Foreign Direct Investment (FDI). Contrastingly, Patrick Minford, member of Economists for Brexit (a group of economists who campaigned to leave, believing in 4% improvement in welfare), believes differently (Emmerson et al., 2016).

The impact on public finances based on NIESR's study is negative, which could wipe out any planned surplus in the short run, and lower GDP per capita in the long run according to economist Richard Portes.

Putting this in context, leaving the EU may lead to an additional two years of austerity measures, such as spending cuts and tax rises, in order to balance the public finances (Emmerson et al., 2016).

"If the long run cost of Brexit is only 3% of GDP as estimated, that represents losing only eighteen months of growth. The global financial crisis of 2008 led to GDP being over 10% lower; therefore, on relative terms, although not insignificant, 3% is not a disaster."

David Miles CBE, Former Member of the MPC

STERLING EXCHANGE RATE

The sterling exchange rate was approximately 20% lower against the US Dollar (USD) immediately following the Brexit vote, dropping from around $1.33 to $1.22. Whilst the devaluation is positive for exports, the impact to the UK is net negative as the UK is a net importer of goods.

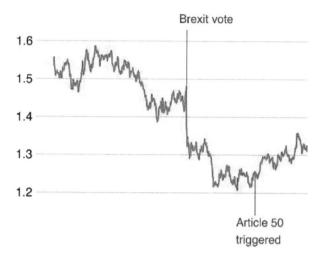

Figure 11a: Pound performance following Brexit result

However, the exchange rate has since recovered to be about 15% lower, which economist David Miles argues is perhaps a necessary correction (given the level of the Current Account Deficit, it is possible the GBP was overvalued). Additionally, a good time to withstand the exchange rate falling is perhaps when inflation is low.

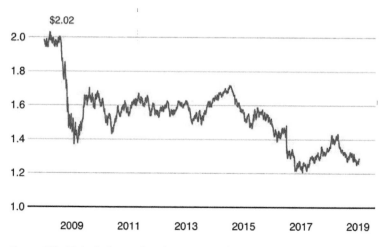

Figure 11b: Historical pound performance against the USD

FOREIGN DIRECT INVESTMENT (FDI)

As the fourth largest recipient of foreign investment after China, the US and Brazil, the UK is seen as the best route to gaining access to the EU (Dhingra et al., 2016b). Foreign direct investment into the UK appears to have reduced due to the heightened uncertainty following the referendum result and investors typically putting a hold on investment plans until there is more clarity.

> "Following Brexit, some investors worry that the UK may behave like an emerging market economy where the government tightens policies to attract foreign investors after a negative shock."
>
> Jacob Nell, Chief UK Economist, Morgan Stanley

With the UK's Current Account Deficit (CAD) at its widest since WWII and the widest in the G10 according to Morgan Stanley research, there is thought among investors about the UK behaving like an Emerging Market (EM). Indicators (such as lower levels of domestic savings) point to a high level of dependence on foreign investor appetite for UK risk.

During an interview in 2016, Jacob Nell suggested that the CAD, combined with the UK's perceived overvalued housing market, is evidence that Brexit may bring significant disruption, and poses a risk of a potential UK break-up, further discouraging investors.

INFLATION

The BoE sets the bank's Monetary Policy Committee (MPC) a 2% target for the annual inflation rate based on the Consumer Prices Index (CPI), in order to maintain stability. The inflation report, produced quarterly, serves as a comprehensive framework for decision-making by MPC members. The indices are produced monthly, and reflect the trend and changes in prices of consumer products.

Following the referendum result, it was expected that there would be weak economic activity, a rise in unemployment due to the uncertainty, and a rise in inflation above the 2% target due to the depreciation of sterling (BoE).

"The weaker sterling resulting in higher inflation could be considered the economic price of Brexit."

David Miles, CBE, Former Member of the MPC

The key economic indicators have recovered from the lows observed immediately after the referendum result, suggesting that the short-run outlook has been stronger than expected, although investment remains subdued. Although the net effect of the long-run impact remains unclear, the overarching perception suggests a negative outlook.

QUANTITATIVE EASING (QE)

Investors believe that QE is a useful tool to fight off recession as the BoE aims to stabilise the economy from the impact of Brexit (Bruce, 2016).

The BoE's bond-buying programme is credited with stabilising the economy following the global financial crisis of 2008. David Miles (former BoE policymaker) argues that bond purchases are most effective when markets are dysfunctional (Bruce, 2016). Following the shock outcome of the 23 June referendum, when the central bank made provision of additional liquidity of up to £250 billion, markets have functioned well according to Mark Carney, the BoE governor (Bruce, 2016).The BoE's response following the referendum results are summarised as follows according to a 2016 Morgan Stanley printed article by Nell et al:

i.   Provision of additional liquidity of up to £250 billion through normal facilities,
ii. Cut in capital requirements through reducing the countercyclical buffer to 0%,
iii. 25 basis points interest rate cut,

iv.   £10 billion corporate bond purchases,

v.   £60 billion gilt purchases (QE), and

vi.   Term Funding Scheme (TFS) (25 basis points four-year funding).

Shortly after the governor of the BoE announced the plan, there were further cuts to interest rates. Lower interest rates lead to a rise in aggregate demand, as the cheaper borrowing and reduced incentive to save can create a ripple effect of increased spending and economic growth.

IMPACT ON FINANCIAL SERVICES

As of early April 2019, we still do not know the terms on which Britain will leave the EU, and there is uncertainty about when it will happen. What we do know is that British firms have been negatively affected by the unprecedented uncertainty created by Brexit. This uncertainty is related to a wide range of government policies, including – but not limited to – foreign trade, immigration, and regulations. Different firms and sectors are affected by Brexit to a different extent and whilst some are hit hard, others seem to be fairly resilient.

The financial services industry appears to be the most exposed to Brexit uncertainty, although the range of potential deals that could be agreed between the UK and the EU are still largely unknown.

Figure 12 illustrates the perceived impact of Brexit on these different sectors of financial services relative to each other as derived from the interviews of leading figures in the industry and research by the author. Impact has been determined based on the industry's activities (such as euro foreign currency trading, investment banking, insurance, and cross-border securities, (Jenkins and Agnew, 2016)) that have thrived since the formation of the Single Market and are therefore most dependent on EU passporting for access.

For a more scientific analysis, Oxford Economics has completed a quantitative research study using their world-class global

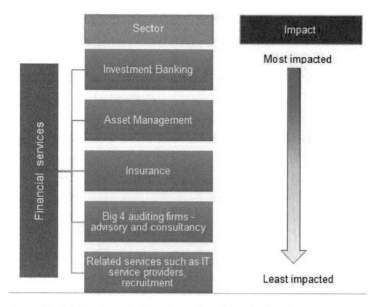

Figure 12: Relative impact of Brexit on financial and related services

economic model. The comprehensive and impartial assessment and data sets based on nine alternative Brexit scenarios provides a full analysis of the implications of Brexit for economic activity in the UK and the rest of the world.

In the paper by authors Paula Hill, Adriana Korczak, and Piotr Korczak of the University of Bristol, the findings indicated that the 'Brexit exposure of financials is 50–60% higher than the exposure of the average firm in the sample. Among financial firms, banks are particularly affected, determined by the ability to serve EU customers from London after Brexit, currently covered by passporting rights as well as the effect of the slowdown in investment by UK companies, reducing the demand for financing'. The authors looked at companies listed on the London Stock Exchange and estimated how Brexit affected their stock prices. According to the findings, 'For the average firm, Brexit is associated with a value loss of 16.4% against a hypothetical no-Brexit scenario.'

Additionally, the findings suggest that multinational firms have been more resilient because the international spread of operations offers a hedge against business exposure in any one market, where operations can be more easily shifted across countries. Examples of internationalisation strategies range from opening foreign subsidiaries to relocating headquarters. According to a recent survey by the Institute of Directors (IoD), 29% of UK companies have relocated (or plan to relocate) some operations abroad due to Brexit uncertainty.

However, 'while internationalisation benefits companies and shareholders, it will negatively impact the UK job market and the economy as a whole', according to Korczak et al.

The consistent themes from the interviews with industry experts are set out below:

DISINTEGRATION

Europe's integrated financial markets have been good for jobs and growth across the continent in the past, and will be good for jobs and growth in the future due to greater efficiency. For example, the integrated financial markets are more efficient, as French farmers, German car manufacturers, and Italian fashion designers can secure funding more easily.

They also contribute to EU citizens receiving better returns on their savings from the increased access to a wider range of products.

ECOSYSTEM EFFECTS

In essence, within the ecosystem a number of related activities may lose the benefits of scale from being part of the ecosystem if the UK leaves the EU, and these activities may also leave the UK. See Insert D for details of the ecosystem dynamic effects.

In addition to the impact arising from the loss of financial services employees, there is also the ecosystem within and between the different financial services and adjacent sectors. Table 5 identifies some of these, including opinions of impact and risk captured during interviews:

Table 5: Ecosystem impacts within the financial services industry

Sector	Ecosystem impacts	Risk
Asset management	Loss of proximity, skills, and reduced liquidity.	Reduction in the value of portfolio management and assets under management delegated to the UK.
Investment banking	Increased fragmentation, capital inefficiency from the cost duplication when EU-related activity is separated from non-EU.	Potential reduction in non-EU clients and related activities.
Specialty insurance	Loss of depth and market expertise if EU-related activities leave the UK.	The UK loses its appeal to international business.

Source: Adapted by author from interview responses

ASSET MANAGEMENT

Asset management has benefitted from cross-border financial services since the formation of the Single Market. Undertakings for Collective Investments in Transferable Securities (UCITS), a cross-border product, have grown and benefitted the UK (Jenkins and Agnew, 2016). Since 2011, net UCITS assets held between the UK, Ireland and Luxembourg have doubled due to cross-border sales (Jenkins and Agnew, 2016).

Following Brexit, the UK may lose its share of UCITS business, worth more than €1 trillion in 2015, to countries located within the EU (Jenkins and Agnew, 2016). According to economist Richard Portes, for businesses where passporting is important, much of the business may be forced into the Eurozone. However, asset managers who do not trade cross-border securities appear to not be too impacted by Brexit.

SPECIALTY INSURANCE

The specialty insurance market Lloyd's of London contributes 20% of the UK financial services GDP, employing 48,000 people (Beale, 2016). London's domination in specialty insurance, namely marine insurance, originated from the seventeenth century. Today's £30 billion market known as Lloyd's of London started in a coffee shop in 1688. The research suggests that following Brexit, some business could shift to other insurance centres such as Singapore (Jenkins and Agnew, 2016). Although this applies broadly, the London-dominated marine market could be most impacted. London currently covers a third of the global marine insurance market worth $18 billion, 40% of which is EU-related (Jenkins and Agnew, 2016).

Writing insurance business across the EU from London through passporting keeps prices low, because having 'to set up local operations across the EU will lead to potential cost increases' (Jenkins and Agnew, 2016).

> *"To think we can still maintain the same access to the Single Market as well as control of the UK Borders is naïve."*
>
> Dr Richard Ward, Former CEO, Lloyd's of London

Contrastingly, 40% of the UK's top insurers believe that Brexit will have limited impact on their business, with 10% stating that Brexit may have a positive impact (EY, 2016).

According to Inga Beale (former CEO, Lloyd's of London), London can still maintain its leading position in specialist insurance and reinsurance by adapting to the new landscape in a post-Brexit environment (Beale, 2016).

> *"Lloyd's will establish a European insurance company in an EU member state."*
>
> Hayley Spink, Brexit Programme Director, Lloyd's of London

INVESTED INSURANCE PREMIUMS

The impact of the referendum on market movements with regards to currency and investments has been dependent on individual firms' strategic investment policy and allocation, and it is therefore inconclusive whether it has had a negative or positive impact so far.

INVESTMENT BANKING

According to British Bankers Association (BBA) Chief Executive Anthony Browne in a speech at the BBA International Banking Conference (2016), Brexit is a challenge for UK-based international banks, if it is to remain equivalent, with no say over regulatory changes, and as a 'rule-taker'. A number of US banks who have set up offices in the UK in order to service their EU clients may now need to plan for the required restructuring if the UK loses access to the Single Market. A successful bilateral market access underpins growth for both the UK and the rest of Europe.

THE DOG THAT DIDN'T BARK

Immediately following the referendum result, banks expected a sharp tightening in financial conditions, but the financial index didn't fall as expected. There was minimal impact and it seemed the markets experienced a loosening of financial conditions instead of a tightening, possibly due to the Bank of England and Bank of Japan both using QE following the Brexit result.

> "In some cases, Brexit was like 'the dog that didn't bark', as the cost of borrowing didn't rise as expected and growth didn't slow."
>
> Jacob Nell, Chief UK Economist, Morgan Stanley

However, in the long run, London's position as one of the leading currency trading hubs could be significantly impacted by Brexit. According to Michael Sherwood, joint head of Goldman Sachs'

European operations until 22 November 2016, revenues increased by up to 60% following a pick-up in business in Europe as a result of the single currency in 1999. Prior to this, most of the banks, including Goldman Sachs, had fragmented trading operations across Europe. Investment banks benefit from the ability to 'passport' around the EU from the UK without needing to set up local operations (Jenkins and Agnew, 2016). This benefit could be jeopardised by Brexit.

> *"In the event of a hard Brexit, banks will need to have a balance sheet within the EU, against which trades can be booked in order to continue to serve EU clients and attract EU businesses for financial services."*
>
> Jacob Nell, Chief UK Economist, Morgan Stanley

FOREIGN EXCHANGE (FOREX) TRADING

Over the last century, although London has dominated currency trading globally, the creation of the EU Single Market and euro in 1999 accelerated trading (Jenkins and Agnew, 2016). Experts claim that the future of euro trading in London is uncertain. For example, in the past the EU's highest court ruled against an attempt by the European Central Bank (ECB) to force the 'clearing and settlement of euro-based transactions into the Eurozone', but with Brexit such a ruling is unlikely (Jenkins and Agnew, 2016).

REGULATORY IMPACT

Key considerations for financial institutions are regulatory and capital requirements, given the pending and recently implemented Regulatory Reform following the global financial crisis of 2008. From the research, whilst it is still unclear what the immediate changes will be once the UK leaves the EU, it is likely that the changes will be significant if the UK is freed from many European regulations. However, there are speculations that the need for banks' capitalisation will be a greater issue in the Brexit run-up and transition.

EQUIVALENCE

There are numerous viewpoints about the equivalence concept, whereby if a country is deemed to have equivalent regulatory standards, then under the 'equivalence regime', they may be able to provide financial services to EU customers. In this scenario the UK becomes a 'rule taker' rather than 'rule maker'. So in effect, the UK may be worse off than remaining in the EU. However, as the UK is a large financial hub, the BoE and Treasury are likely to insist on having some control (HM Treasury, 2016). Therefore, equivalence will be an inadequate substitute due to:

i.   a narrower range of services,
ii. being a rule taker and not a rule maker,
iii. the BoE insisting on making rules.

However, according to a *CityWire* article by David Campbell, as part of Theresa May's Chequers deal, the UK will seek an enhanced version of the regulatory equivalence recognition which currently governs financial services sold into the EU from third countries. This is a critical consideration for the following reasons:

- The funds industry would be one of many areas of the financial services industry likely to face serious challenges on the first day after Brexit.
- UK consumers are likely to be mainly impacted by more expensive and burdensome cross-border payment costs, whilst UK pensioners in the EU may face difficulties accessing annuities and insurance products.
- Capital market participants face the potential loss of a legal and regulatory framework in settling contracts.

The Potential Impact of the Single Market Access Scenarios

The two potential outcomes of any agreement, according to Oliver Wyman research, will either lead to a:

i.   High-access scenario, or
ii. Low-access scenario.

HIGH-ACCESS SCENARIO

In this scenario, the UK will be deemed to have regulatory equivalence across a broad range of existing EU legislation. However, new agreements may be required in areas with no existing provisions for access to third countries, for example the Capital Requirements Directive (CRD) and the Insurance Distribution Directive (IDD) may be impacted.

LOW-ACCESS SCENARIO

In this scenario, the UK may move to a third country position with the EU, with limited recognition of regulatory equivalence and restrictions on Eurozone activities that could be carried out. This will result in increased costs from the lengthy operational set-up and required licensing of new legal entities.

Table 6 sets out the key challenges of a low-access scenario:

Table 6: Challenges associated with setting up a base inside the EU

Operational set-up of new legal entities	The complexity of the various financial services' sectors means that businesses are reliant on robust operational processes and technology. Developing the required architecture for new legal entities may take several years.
Licensing	Relocating offices require licenses to operate in new jurisdictions. A rigorous regulatory review process could take up to eighteen months and possibly longer, if large parts of the sector migrate.

Internal model approvals	Most financial institutions require risk models to be approved by the local regulators. Obtaining a model 'sign-off' could take years through iterative dialogue with regulators.
Capital release and redeployment	Moving business and capital between two legal entities may not be simultaneous. Regulatory requirements by the local regulator may need to be satisfied before capital can be released. In effect, this may result in the company having to hold twice as much capital for a period of time and therefore leading to inefficient use of capital.
Skills and training	Developing similar talent pools in other European cities could take several years given the specialist nature of the sector which has developed in London over decades.
Infrastructure	The infrastructure supporting London's role as a financial centre has developed over decades, including office locations, international airports, schools and other related facilities. This could take several years to be reproduced in another EU city.

Source: Adapted by author from interviews and Oliver Wyman research

Firms may be unable to serve EU clients when the new rules come into force if they fail to make the necessary changes on time. As a result, most institutions are making contingency plans for both high- and low-access scenarios.

Drivers of Brexit

A critical assessment of the rationale behind the referendum result provides a good basis for understanding the various sectoral impacts and the UK's options. Whilst the focus of this book has been from an economic perspective, the political impact has been inescapable. Therefore, it is necessary to understand some of the political, as well as economic, drivers that led to the Brexit result.

DISENCHANTMENT

There are numerous findings, suggesting that austerity was a key driver for the 'Leave' result according to Thiemo Fetzer, an Associate Professor in the economics department of the University of Warwick. To provide a complete view, the drivers of the referendum result were analysed. These included factors such as the perception of immigration. There is limited evidence to support the view that immigration has negatively impacted employment. The unemployment rate is currently less than 5% (Trading Economics). Indeed, the UK has one of the highest employment rates in a developed economy.

For balance, I have analysed some of the claims about the impact of immigration on employment as a motivation for the Brexit camp.

Figure 13 indicates that immigration has had a positive impact on GDP and the UK's standard of living. As illustrated in the below chart in brown and green bars, non-EU and EU-born employees appear to have had a positive contribution to the change in total employment and GDP growth.

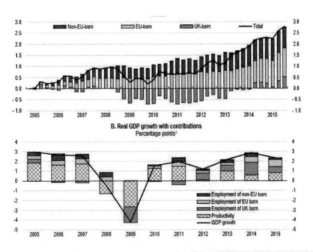

ScatLink ᴸᶦⁿᵏ *http://dx.doi.org/10.1787/888933351127*

1. The sum of contributions of employment growth by country of birth does not equal the sum of total employment as the series for total employment also includes people who do not state their country of birth or nationality.

Source: ONS (2016), "UK Labour Market: March 2016", *Statistical Bulletin*, Office for National Statistics; and OECD (2016), *OECD Economic Outlook: Statistics and Projections* (database), April.

Figure 13: The impact of immigration on employment and GDP growth in the UK

Additionally, it is worth noting that employees who are UK-born had a higher contribution to real GDP between 2012 and 2014, although a negative contribution was observed in 2009 following the global financial crisis of 2008.

COST – BENEFIT

As stated in Chapter 1, a significant proportion of the population voted to leave, and their rationale was not necessarily down to anti-immigration or xenophobic sentiments, but rather people voted to change the status quo based on the cost and benefit of the EU membership. As a significant contributor to the EU budget, some respondents believed that the UK's voice in the EU was not proportional to its contribution. This view is further supported by economist David Miles as reported by Bower in 2016: 'There was a fairly rational cost-benefit analysis that may have gone through the minds of many people who voted to leave.' It appears that the same issue with regards to the negotiating power of the UK continues to play out through the withdrawal agreement negotiations. At the time of writing, Prime Minister Theresa May is yet to secure an acceptable deal after three defeats. Two of these were historical Commons defeats, where MPs rejected her deal by 432 to 202 votes in January 2019 and by 391 to 242 votes in March 2019. The deal had taken over two years to negotiate, and there had also been resignations of two Brexit Secretaries in that period.

"There was a fairly rational cost-benefit analysis that may have gone through the minds of many people who voted to leave."

David Miles, CBE, Former Member of the MPC

THE CITY 'BREXITEERS'

Interestingly, given the potential negative impact of Brexit on the financial services industry, there were a number of Brexit supporters from this industry, although most seem to be within the asset management industry. This is surprising, because one of the most tangible successes in EU cross-border services are UCITS funds.

In summary, according to an article by Scot James, Senior Lecturer in Political Economy at King's College London, Brexit has had a varied impact across the financial services industry – between the banking and non-banking sectors. Warren et al, found that large global investment banks, which rely heavily on 'passporting' into the EU Single Market, were highly vocal in pushing for 'Remain'. On the other hand, UK-focused retail banks were more concerned to avoid the UK becoming a 'rule taker' from Brussels in the future, while other parts of the financial sector (notably insurance and hedge funds) viewed Brexit as an opportunity to roll back burdensome regulations.

In the following chapter I discuss the UK's options for Brexit.

CHAPTER 4

The UK's Options

The UK's various options at a high level are set out in Figure 14 and further discussed in the following pages. It is worth noting that almost all of the Brexit options were rejected by the Members of Parliament in the indicative votes held on 27 March 2019.

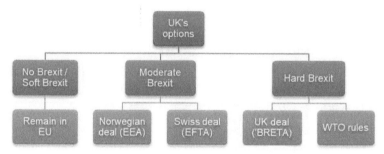

Figure 14: The UK's options

See Insert E for a more detailed illustration of the UK's various options and the estimated net EU budgetary contribution associated with each.

MODERATE BREXIT: NORWEGIAN DEAL (EEA)

A soft to moderate Brexit implies continued access to the Single Market, but with no control over EU migration, this option is described as 'Norway Minus', according to economist Jacob Nell. The case of a Norway-type agreement suggests that the UK's net EU budget contributions could be significantly lower if the UK left the EU and joined the EEA (Emmerson et al., 2016).

Whilst this moderate option appears to be the least economically damaging, further research suggests this may be an unrealistic option with the decreased scope to influence EU policies, in the capacity as a 'rule taker'. On 27 March, MPs voted by 377 to 65 votes to reject this option.

MODERATE BREXIT: SWISS DEAL (EFTA)

This option, also known as 'Norway Plus' or 'Common Market 2.0', would involve the UK joining Norway, Iceland, Switzerland and Liechtenstein as part of the European Free Trade Association (EFTA). Switzerland is part of the EFTA instead of the EEA, which allows free access to the EU's manufactured goods market, but with limited access to services. Switzerland has negotiated a series of deals with the EU for specific sectors, such as insurance, which still leaves out several financial services (Emmerson et al., 2016). Some Swiss organisations have been able to get round this until now by having a branch in the UK.

The Swiss deal will not be a suitable option for the UK, as Swiss banks cannot provide investment banking services to their clients from Switzerland and have relied on having an office in the UK. On 27 March, MPs voted by 283 to 188 votes to reject the Common Market 2.0 option.

"Brexit presents no easy options."

Hayley Spink, Brexit Programme Director, Lloyd's of London

Hard Brexit Options

The findings from my research suggest that the likelihood of a hard Brexit is predicted to be between 60–70% in 2016, and almost three years later, UK Trade Secretary Liam Fox put the likelihood of failing to reach an agreement at 60%. The three rejections of Mrs May's deal so far is a strong indication of a potential 'no-deal' exit, despite the votes to nullify that option.

The two possible options for a hard Brexit are:

i.   WTO rules, and
ii. Customised UK Trade agreement ('BRETA').

HARD BREXIT OPTION 1: WTO RULES (NO-DEAL)

In the event of a 'no-deal', the UK may default to World Trade Organization (WTO) rules. The rules include no free movement within the EU, no financial contribution to it, and no obligation to apply EU laws. However, traded goods would still need to adhere to EU standards, with some tariffs in place on other EU trades. Additionally, access to services would be restricted as WTO rules have no meaningful provision for financial services according to Jacob Nell, Chief Economist of Morgan Stanley.

It is important that the UK remains a competitive business location for international banks for a more positive jobs and growth prospect. Therefore, it is advisable for the industry and government to make transitional arrangements, so that customers can access financial services before the new UK–EU partnership agreement comes into force.

This option may be costly and disruptive to organisations, thus contributing to a negative impact overall for the UK by displacing some activities from the UK to other jurisdictions, according to Jacob Nell.

Under this no-deal scenario, after leaving the EU, the UK is assumed to trade simply under WTO rules, without seeking a new trade agreement with the EU or other trading partners like the United States. The UK would simply pay the external tariffs. This is usually the worst-case scenario that other economists have modelled. An analysis by HM Treasury in 2016, for example, finds a GDP drop of 7.5% under this scenario.

As part of the Treasury's contingency plan, whatever the outcome of the Brexit negotiations, 'it was increasing readiness for other scenarios', such as handing additional rule-making powers previously held by EU bodies to UK regulators and establishing a licensing regime to allow European companies to continue to operate.

With the likelihood of a no-deal estimated at 60%, some of the leading Brexiteers in the financial sector have cheered the prospect of a hard, fast break from the EU, according to David Campbell, reporting for *CityWire*. The Prime Minister's voice cracked as she made a final plea with MPs to back her Brexit deal, as "Brexit could be lost" if MPs reject her Withdrawal Agreement once again, on 12th March. Coughing and clearing her throat, the PM immediately made a joke about what appears to be the same ailment that overshadowed her speech during the Conservative Party conference in 2017. In response to jeers from the opposition, the PM quipped: "OK, ...you should hear Jean-Claude Juncker's voice as a result of our conversation." She was making reference to Brexit discussions with the President of the European Commission, which ran into the early hours, as she tried to find a way out of the Brexit impasse that has divided Parliament.

However, following another historical rejection of the deal on 12 March 2019 (although marginally better than the first defeat on 15 January 2019), the Prime Minister who appears to have lost her voice literally and metaphorically, addressed the House about the intentions of the Conservative party to offer its MPs a free vote on a no-deal exit the following day (MPs voted by 400 to 160 votes against no-deal). This was followed by a vote on an extension of Article 50 the day after, following the positive outcome of the vote against a no-deal exit. The second rejection of the withdrawal agreement was anticipated following the Attorney General's (AG) earlier announcement concerning the Northern Ireland backstop: 'That there has been no change to the legal risk that the UK could be stuck in the withdrawal agreement indefinitely.' The concern about the Northern Ireland backstop and why the Democratic Unionist Party loathed the deal, is because it 'effectively granted the EU a veto over the UK's exit in assurances on the free flow of goods across the Irish border'. The AG emphasised this point in an address to Parliament.

The capital markets were down following the AG's announcement, creating a new level of uncertainty that resulted in businesses appealing to MPs to move quickly to take no-deal off the table. In her speech, following the second and third defeat of her deal, the PM acknowledged the grave importance of the decision based on strongly held and equally legitimate views on both sides. However, she recommended that the UK leave in an orderly way with a deal, as leaving without a deal would be catastrophic. In light of this, and at the time of writing it seemed a longer extension may be necessary.

CONTINGENCY PLANS

In preparation for the possibility of a no-deal, of which UK Trade Secretary Liam Fox puts the chances at 60%, large financial institutions have shifted, or are planning to shift, billions of pounds' worth of assets into the EU – £166 billion in Barclays' case, as reported by Robin Amos for *CityWire*. These plans were approved by the High Court as part of implementing contingency plans for a no-deal Brexit. To put this in context, this represents around 15% of the £1.1 trillion in assets the bank held at the end of 2017.

However, most financial institutions, including Barclays, will be able to use existing licensed EU-based bank subsidiaries to continue to serve clients within the EU after Brexit.

Additionally, the UK regulator – the Financial Conduct Authority (FCA) – recently published more information to help firms prepare for Brexit, including updated advice on preparations, rules, and guidance that will apply in a no-deal scenario, further details on the temporary transition power, and how firms will be affected.

SETTLED STATUS

The Institute of Directors (IoD) published an article titled 'What will happen to EU nationals living and working in the UK as a result of Brexit?' The report highlighted that there are over three million citizens of other EU member states living in the UK, the majority of whom work in critical roles. This is a major concern for UK companies to protect the right of their EU staff remaining in the UK after Brexit. As part of the contingency planning, the UK government has initiated the EU settlement scheme referred to as 'Settled Status', which must be applied for as it is not granted automatically. Broadly all EU citizens living in the UK and their families and dependents must apply for 'Settled Status', except for those who have already become British citizens or have received indefinite leave to enter, or remain, in the UK. The *settled status* scheme, which forms part of the withdrawal agreement with the EU, if ratified, must be applied for by 30 June 2021.

Further details can be found from the Home Office, which has provided a number of resources for businesses impacted.

HARD BREXIT OPTION 2: UK DEAL ('BRETA')

There are two implications of the referendum result: political and economic. My research results from 2016, which is still relevant, indicated a higher likelihood for a hard Brexit or a new UK–EU agreement. Businesses are in a unique position, as the referendum result means the UK now has the opportunity to define new trading agreements with its trading partners. This has created the potential for businesses to maximise the opportunities a new trading model will present whilst minimising any negative impacts on their business model and the UK economy, as discussed in Chapter 2.

However, the existing UK–EU withdrawal agreement, currently referred to as Prime Minister Theresa May's deal, has been historically rejected twice (MPs voted by 432 to 202 votes in January 2019 and 391 to 242 votes in March 2019 against Mrs May's deal). Mrs May indicated she will stand down before the next phase of Brexit negotiations, if the deal was accepted when presented for the third time.

29th March 2019, on the day the UK was originally supposed to leave the EU, MPs voted for a third time on the twice-rejected Theresa May's withdrawal agreement, although it was slightly different this time. The Brexit deal had two main elements:

i.   the legally binding withdrawal agreement which covers money, the transition period, citizens' rights and the Northern Ireland border; and,
ii. the political declaration about the long-term future relationship between the UK and the EU.

MPs voted on half of it – the withdrawal agreement alone, which covers the divorce settlement – rather than both the withdrawal agreement and the political declaration. This was to satisfy the conditions set by John Bercow, the Speaker of the House of Commons, that another vote on the deal could not be brought if it was 'substantially the same'. Additionally, the agreement with the EU only required MPs to approve the withdrawal agreement to allow the longer delay to 22 May if successful.

Prime Minister Theresa May's deal was defeated for the third time when MPs voted by 344 to 286 votes to reject the withdrawal agreement. This result came as no surprise, as the BBC political editor Laura Kuenssberg stated prior to the vote that it 'looks like Mrs May is heading for another loss'. The Northern Irish DUP had stated that it would not support it, because of the Irish backstop, and most Labour MPs were also expected to vote against, as stated by Sir Keir Starmer, the Shadow Brexit Secretary. It appeared that Mrs May's deal was being rejected because, it had been described as BRINO – Brexit In Name Only.

Following the third defeat of the deal, it appeared there were still several possible outcomes. With Mrs May offering to stand down if her deal had been supported, and potentially planning to present it a fourth time, there was the prospect of a Conservative leadership contest, which may necessitate delaying the UK's departure from the EU further.

CETA AS A PRECEDENT

The EU has most recently completed a free trade deal with Canada, called the Comprehensive Economic and Trade Agreement (CETA), where Canada has agreed to better conditions for EU companies compared to companies outside the EU (European Union, 2016). This Canadian model sets a good precedent for the UK to negotiate a similar agreement, which could be called the British Economic and Trade Agreement ('BRETA'). CETA appears to be the most comprehensive free trade agreement that the EU has agreed to date, providing tariff- and quota-free access for significant areas of services with some exceptions for financial services (European Union, 2016). However, a key consideration is that there are no budgetary contributions to the EU, although the degree of Canada's trade with the EU is likely to be less than the UK, at least from a geographical perspective given the proximity between both. For some of these reasons the EU–Canada deal is perhaps not a perfect template for a bespoke British trade model. However, it is noteworthy, as it sets out the range of trade agreements signed by the EU and non-members, and the schedule of budget contributions. For example, the EEA countries with the highest access to the single market are required to contribute grants to the poorer parts of the EU. Whilst the contribution to the EU programmes could be substantial it would be less than the current UK net contributions (Baker et al., 2016).

"It may take up to ten years to complete a new UK trade deal."
Jacob Nell, Chief UK Economist, Morgan Stanley

Summary

The impact of Brexit on the UK's financial services sector will depend on the level of access retained to the EU as well as between the different financial services sectors. Several institutions have indicated that the cost of relocation and the inefficiencies resulting from the fragmented operations could lead to scale backs or closure of parts of the business.

I believe that the optimal Brexit scenario will be neither 'soft' nor 'hard', and as we move towards accepting that Brexit is inevitable, it is advisable that the UK and EU government explore constructive ways to structure and agree what Brexit becomes in order to minimise the disruption for UK businesses.

> "No one knows what Brexit means and this means uncertainty. The financial markets like certainty."
>
> Dr Richard Ward, former CEO, Lloyd's of London

The economic impact of Brexit depends on the policies the UK adopts. Lower trade from reduced integration may cost the UK economy more than is gained from reduced contributions to the EU budget (Dhingra et al., 2016a).

Although the inescapable political debate is out of the scope of this research, the UK may come out of this stronger given the current political uncertainties in some of the other European countries. Additionally, with the increasing anti-establishment rhetoric, there may be other countries exiting the EU after the UK. If that happens, the UK may be in a much stronger position to negotiate and agree new trade agreements. It is both in the UK's and the EU's best interests to agree a deal that is mutually beneficial. In this context, this presents an opportunity for the UK to define a customised 'Brit model' that satisfies the issues that led to the Brexit vote as much as possible as well as maintaining the economic growth and existing standard of living.

See Insert E for an illustration of the UK's possible trade options and estimated net EU contributions for each option.

The following chapter sets out recommendations for the UK government and businesses based on the summary of the research findings.

CHAPTER 5

Recommendations

Set out in the table below are some recommendations for the key features in any future UK–EU agreement to ensure the optimal levels of employment and services delivered to consumers, both within the UK and across the EU.

Table 7: Brexit recommendations for the UK Government

Time frame	Feature and Recommendation	Mutual Benefits
UK Government		
Short-term	Orderly transition	
	• The UK government, as part of its negotiation, should aim to provide clear direction for an orderly transition following the finalisation of the terms of exit.	• More stable markets.
		• Reassures consumers.
	• Communicate the transition time frame using 'forward guidance' to stem the uncertainty in the markets as soon as possible.	• Minimises restructuring costs from reduced uncertainty.
	• Partner with financial services lobby groups to define a transition window whereby the continuation of services to customers can be as seamless as possible as the sector implements the required changes to operating models.	
Medium- to Long-term	Maintaining as close to current access to the international markets as possible	
	• Maintain some access to the Single Market and other international markets, but not as a member of the EU, but rather similar to Norway's deal for a reduced contribution and better control of the borders.	• Access to the Single Market will keep the Eurozone as integrated as possible, as any perceived benefits from fragmentation are limited.
	• Maintain, as much as is feasible, any recognised equivalence granted as part of EU membership with non-EU nations after leaving the EU.	

Trade deal

- CETA provides a good reference point with regards to the UK being able to sign a deal that will maintain its leading financial services status.

  - The UK can maintain its leading position in global financial services with internal capitals based in the UK.

Immigration

- Assuage the anti-immigration sentiments without reducing the degree of free movement too significantly.
- Implement an annual complementary high-skilled visa quota system based on priority businesses' requirements where there is a skills shortage.

  - Reduced cost of fragmentation and withdrawal of talent from the UK.

Grandfathering of regulatory equivalence status

- Equivalence agreements should be 'grandfathered', especially in key directives where the UK shares common rules with the EU such as:
  - Alternative Investment Fund Managers Directive (AIFMD)
  - Capital Requirement Directive IV (CRD IV)
  - European Market Infrastructure Regulation (EMIR)
  - Markets in Financial Instruments Directive (MiFID I & II)
  - Solvency II (SII)
  - Payment Services Directive II (PSD II)
  - Insurance Distribution Directive (IDD)

  - Maintain reciprocal access to the Single Market between EU and UK.
  - Reduce additional costs from 'contingency plans' and loss of services to customers.

Long-term

Education: training and skills

- The UK currently has a high number of the world's leading institutions and therefore has the capability and resource to produce more Science, Technology, Engineering and Mathematics (STEM) graduates.
- Encourage more STEM subjects through incentivising with, perhaps, lower university fees. For example, £9,000 per year for other subjects and reduced scale, say £6,000, to produce more STEM graduates. Given the CAD, this could be funded from the savings to EU contribution or reduced overseas aid.

- Close skills shortage gap.
- Increase employment level.

Table 8: Recommendations to UK-based businesses

UK-based Businesses

Time frame	Feature	Recommendation	Mutual benefit
Short- to Medium-term	Assess vulnerability	Assess business links and exposure to the EU.	Set out a clear plan to mitigate any identified vulnerabilities.
		Set out potential transition period timescales.	To limit disruption following the triggering of Article 50.
Medium-term	Regulation	Examine possible consequences of taxation, regulation, and immigration in existing trade contracts.	To provide clarity about contractual relationships and obligations in a post-Brexit environment.
Medium- to Long-term	Trade negotiation	Lobby governmental institutions in order to try to achieve the optimal access to the Single Market.	In a high-access scenario with a clear and sensible transition period, the disruption could be negligible.
			Enables the UK to maximise the potential growth opportunities that could arise from the UK's exit from the EU.

CONCLUSION?

Over the course of this book, several studies have assessed some aspects of the economic impact of leaving the EU. Although the Brexit vote was intended to be advisory, it has become a mandate and an invidious task for Prime Minister Theresa May. At the time of writing, Brexit appears to be getting more complex by the day as not only is it literally consuming MPs, it is also consuming a lot of airtime by poisoning the political well as the MPs appear to be more divided. There is still some degree of uncertainty as the experts do not agree, and have a variegated view of the UK's future economic prospects. Leading international and economic development organisations, such as the International Monetary Fund (IMF) and the Organisation for Economic Co-operation and Development (OECD), have contributed to the debate, whilst the BoE has taken measures to ensure financial stability.

Whilst some findings provide clear evidence of gains or losses from Brexit, others illustrate the cost of uncertainty and its resulting impact on the British economy over the last three years. Whilst claims from leading economists (including George Osborne, the former Chancellor of the Exchequer) that house prices may fall perhaps by as much as 20%, may or may not be correct, it will be good news for those currently unable to step on to the housing ladder, yet bad for the serial property investors. There are several similar distributive effects, whether in relation to income, jobs, or other influences on well-being.

There have been many attempts to model the macroeconomic consequences of Brexit, nearly all of which find that there will be a long-term loss of GDP for the UK economy compared with the status quo projections of remaining fully in the EU and its Single Market. It is important to stress that this means lower GDP than would otherwise be the case, not an actual fall in prosperity.

The Prospects of No-deal

There are two schools of thought when it comes to analysing the consequences of a no-deal scenario. As an eternal optimist, let me start with the good news.

A no-deal Brexit could be the 'best option' for the UK after it leaves the European Union. This theory is also supported by Hargreaves Lansdown co-founder, Peter Hargreaves, as reported in *CityWire*. The main reason given for this optimistic outlook is that the largest EU economies other than the UK – Germany, France, and Italy – are huge exporters to the UK, and are therefore likely to 'demand free trade from the EU'.

In terms of the bad news, according to an article published by *The Economist*, no-deal amounts to a very bad deal, as it would rip up forty-five years of arrangements with a vital ally. 'Reneging on £39 billion ($50 billion) in obligations to the EU would impair Britain's international credibility'. Additionally, a no-deal on the Irish border would 'test the Good Friday Agreement that ended a serious armed conflict'. However, 'no-dealers' argue that Britain could eventually adjust to the new normal.

Importantly, no-deal would mean not just no trade deal, but the dislocation of 'a whole corpus of legal arrangements with the

EU', according to *The Economist*. What some Brexiteers describe as a 'clean break' from Europe could in fact be rather messy.

In the evening of 29 March 2019 (the UK's original departure date), there were protest marches through London as the EU was yet to reach an agreement on a deal that would be acceptable to the UK. Following the failures to get her Brexit deal through Parliament, Prime Minister Theresa May wrote to EU Council President Donald Tusk requesting a Brexit delay to 30 June. In response, Donald Tusk said that, 'EU27 agreed to offer the UK an extension to Brexit until May 22, if MPs approve Theresa May's withdrawal agreement. However, as the Prime Minister's withdrawal agreement was voted down, the UK had until April 12 to outline its next steps.' The extension to 22 May was partly due to the European Parliament elections being held between 23–26 May. The European elections had to be held in a clear framework, and strict legal interpretation dictated that if the UK was not taking part, then they will have to have left the EU. In contrast to previous years, there appeared to be increased interest in the European Parliamentary elections. Some commentators have stated that given the current impasse in the House, this election was being treated as a proxy referendum on Brexit.

The news of the first extension was well received by the markets, with the pound strengthening after falling the day before on the prospect of a no-deal exit. Though, it does seem ironic that what was supposed to be about getting back power appears to have resulted in the UK being weaker. It was also interesting to read the report of Prime Minister Theresa May left waiting while EU leaders decided the UK's fate behind closed doors with regards to the extension request. The Prime Minister had hoped for an extension until 30 June but instead received a 'complicated conditional plan'. This image of the UK Prime Minister waiting outside the room may symbolise the post-Brexit landscape, if the claims and commentaries from the critics are anything to go by. However, with the benefit of hindsight, perhaps it provides some perspective of the consequences. It appears, according to Ivan Rogers, the UK's former ambassador to the EU, 'that in taking back control over our law we are privileging notional autonomy over real power to set the rules by which in practice we shall be governed – since we will no longer be in the room'. Rogers states that 'the EU is a global player, a global rule maker – able and willing to impose its values, rules and standards extraterritorially'.

The landscape remains unsettled, likened to quicksand, with conflicting analyses making it difficult to judge who is (or is most likely to be) right about the outlook for the UK when it leaves the EU. MPs approved (by 441 to 105 votes in favour) the secondary legislation to change the date of Brexit in UK law. It means the new legal date for the UK's departure would have been 22 May, had the PM's deal been approved by the Commons. However, as it was rejected the third time, the new date for Brexit was set for 12 April by EU leaders to provide more time to get a deal through, or for the UK to 'indicate a way forward'. Indicative votes were held on 27 March for a series of eight alternative Brexit options, and on 1 April for a series of four options, as set out in Table 9.

Table 9 – Series of alternative Brexit options voted on by MPs

Brexit Options	27 March		1 April	
	Voted For	Voted Against	Voted For	Voted Against
No deal	160	400	N/A	N/A
Customs union	265	271	273	276
Common Market 2.0	189	283	261	282
EFTA and EEA	65	377	N/A	N/A
Revocation to avoid no deal	184	293	N/A	N/A
Contingent preferential arrangements	139	422	N/A	N/A
Confirmatory public vote	268	295	280	292

Labour's alternative plan	237	307	N/A	N/A
Parliamentary supremacy	N/A	N/A	191	292

As can be seen in Table 9, the indicative votes had no overall majority for any of the series of eight alternative Brexit options. However, it is worth highlighting that the Customs Union and confirmatory public vote (alternatively referred to as the People's Vote) came closest to securing a majority in both rounds, and the Common Market 2.0 (during the second round) with the margins narrowing respectively. Although close to six million signatures were received on a petition to revoke Article 50, cancelling Brexit was not an option. As set out in the table, MPs voted by 293 to 184 votes to reject this option.

In light of the above indicative votes results, the UK can only hope for the best in leaving with a deal that moves the country forward, and also prepare for the worst in the event of an accidental no-deal crash exit.

THE 'FLEXTENSION'

With the results from the second round of indicative votes yielding no majority either, (although the Customs Union option achieved the narrowest margin) Mrs May reached out to the leader of the opposition, Jeremy Corbyn, a meeting most members of her cabinet did not approve of. However, Mrs May was keen on reaching some agreement or plan by the 12 April deadline set by the EU. Following which, Mrs May wrote to the President of the EU Council, Donald Tusk, requesting an extension to 30 June for the second time, even after senior EU officials had indicated that the EU was willing to offer a flexible extension – flextension – of up to 12 months, till 29 March 2020, which could be reduced if an agreement was reached sooner.

Whilst it may have seemed ambitious and sent the right signals to the majority of the electorate, for the PM to only request an extension until 30 June, was, experts suggested, to avoid the UK potentially taking part in the European Parliament elections. The outcome of which had been predicted to be unfavourable for the Prime Minister, in light of the impasse, not to mention that elected officials may not have taken their seats, in the event that the UK were to leave the EU before the revised deadline of 31 October 2019.

In response to Mrs May's second extension request, European Council President Donald Tusk confirmed the EU's offer of a new delay to Brexit until 31 October 2019, with a review of progress to be held in June. Described as a 'flexible' extension to Article 50, the UK would be able to exit earlier if the withdrawal agreement was ratified by Parliament.

This October cut-off would mean the UK would leave before the next EU Commission took office on 1 November, thus limiting the UK's entanglement in the next phase of EU business.

As at 12 April (the alternative expected no-deal Brexit date), 'no deal' preparations were being wound down with immediate effect according to the government.

So with a new Brexit extension, allowing more time to either ratify the existing deal or define new terms, with the MPs voting to reject most, if not all, of the Brexit options tabled so far, the question that must be answered by the set deadline is – what does the UK want?

What Does the UK Want?

In my opinion, the story of the UK joining the EU in the first place as discussed in Chapter 1 and now wanting to leave can be likened to the Founder's Dilemma. The Founder's Dilemma is a concept popularised by Noam Wasserman, a professor at Harvard Business School. This describes how entrepreneurs or founders often make decisions that conflict with the wealth-maximisation principle in order to maintain control. In essence, there is a trade-off between maintaining control – as in 'King' – or giving up control to maximise wealth. The idea is that for a venture to increase its market share, at some point the founders will invite outsiders to invest in their company. In doing so, they may have to give up total control over the running of the company. Control is transferred to a Board of Directors, and outside directors also join the company's board. Once the founder is no longer in control of the board, his or her job as CEO is at risk.

Although this theory appears to be quite a stretch, there are however some points of similarity. The Harvard research shows that a founder who gives up more equity to attract investors builds a more valuable company where the founder ends up with a more valuable slice too. However, this comes at a price, as in order to attract investors, the founders have to give up control over most of the decision-making. Noam asserts that 'this fundamental tension yields "rich" versus "king" trade-offs'. The 'rich' choice isn't necessarily better than a 'king' choice or vice versa; what matters is how well each decision fits with the founder's desires.

Choosing between money and power allows entrepreneurs to come to grips with what success means to them. Founders who want to manage empires will not believe they are successes if they lose control, even if they end up rich.

In order to answer the question – what does the UK want? – I suspect the answer is somewhere between both being 'king' and 'rich'. Therefore, the best outcome for the UK, irrespective of the economic impact, will be based on which is most important for the electorate. It seems in 1973 when the UK had relatively weak economic performance compared to other European countries, being 'rich' was a priority and hence why the UK joined the EU in the first place. However, being 'king' appears to be more important now.

According to Ivan Rogers, the UK's former ambassador to the EU, 'the sovereigntist argument for Brexit… taking back control of laws, borders and money… was one powerful element of the referendum campaign'. However, it has since become apparent that the UK cannot have 'all the benefits of staying in a Customs Union with the EU whilst leaving it to have a fully sovereign trade policy'. Thus, the trade-offs between 'rich' versus 'king' are 'real and difficult'.

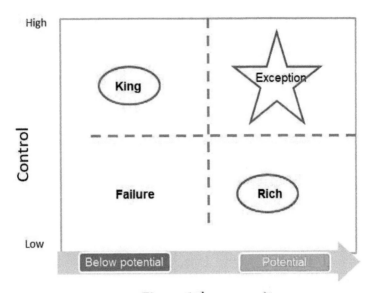

Figure 15: The Founder's Dilemma, 'Rich' or 'King'?

Figure 15 is an illustration of the framework introduced by Noam Wasserman for solving the Founder's Dilemma, and could be useful in answering the question, *What does the UK want – 'king' or 'rich'?* There are of course some case study examples, where being both 'king' and 'rich' is possible, such as with Bill Gates of Microsoft, Phil Knight of Nike, and The Body Shop's Anita Roddick, but these are very rare examples.

Figure 15 indicates that where there's complete control, as in 'king' – the relative level of financial prosperity is below potential, and it is usually the exception to have full control and still achieve the full financial prosperity potential. On the flip side, little control and still achieving below potential will be classified as a 'failure' of sovereignty. On the bottom right of the quadrant, we find that, to be 'rich' – benefitting from the full financial prosperity potential – requires some loss of control.

Even with the extended deadline, some experts believe

that the UK may not leave the EU on time, not least because of the 'volume of legislation that must still be passed', according to Chancellor Phillip Hammond. MPs have voted against leaving the EU without a deal, and have thrice rejected the Prime Minister's deal. With a Conservative leadership contest imminent following the resignation of Prime Minister Theresa May, the key to any new deal being acceptable could be linked to the answer to the question – does the UK want to be 'king' or 'rich'?

As the UK is fast approaching the end game with the EU, are there any strategic moves left to play before it is 'checkmate'? Given the perceived weak opening move and some other unexpected moves in between, such as triggering Article 50 without a plan, and Prime Minister Theresa May offering her resignation in order to try to secure support for her deal the third time, what else is still left to play to satisfy the electorate? Could no-deal have been the end game, or are there other more unexpected twists and turns before the UK or EU are in checkmate, and one of them is crowned 'king', irrespective of the economic and social consequences?

Let me take a moment to apply my learnings about negotiation on the no-deal scenario, which appears to have increased in likelihood. The essence of a negotiation is to know your walk-away value, known as the Best Alternative To A Negotiated Agreement (BATNA). In this case, perhaps 'no-deal' could have been the UK's BATNA – whilst it carries a high risk, the other side of the negotiation are probably more apprehensive about a no-deal Brexit. This is supported by reports of the German Chancellor Angela Merkel visiting Northern Ireland in a bid to try to prevent a no-deal, pledging to 'do everything she can to prevent no-deal Brexit.' On that basis, whether it's considered a bluff or not, it may have strengthened the UK's negotiating position (although easier said than done). However, that is the art of negotiation: the other side believing you can walk away if they can't offer a deal that is agreeable. Of course, it all boils down to who has the most to lose, which would determine whether 'no-deal' is indeed a credible BATNA, and then ensuring the downside of the BATNA is mitigated.

Given that Brexit was not about economic benefits, we may already have the answer. But can the UK have both, be 'king' and 'rich', thus satisfying both the 51.9% who voted to leave, and the 48.1% who voted to remain? This outcome may not be impossible, but unrealistic and akin to 'having your cake and eating it'.

However, there have been some breakthroughs, with customs concessions likely to be agreed as long as a hard Irish border can be avoided. It would appear that the United Kingdom is somewhat divided, and with the topic of Brexit becoming even more invidious, 'a house divided against itself cannot stand'. Therefore, a key objective to any deal that is eventually agreed (irrespective of who delivers it) should be one that mends and brings the country together.

To try to end on a bright note, there is some recent news of Norwegians planning to invest billions in the UK. According to *The Times* 'the world's largest sovereign wealth fund is taking a 30-year bet that Britain will emerge from Brexit stronger outside the European Union'. Therefore, with employment levels at a record high, a potential to agree to a better deal, and with the 'benefit of hindsight' over the last three years where economic performance has exceeded expectations, it appears that some of the doom and gloom forecast prior to and on the morning of the referendum result has not materialised, at least not yet. If this is anything to go by, it is therefore not entirely preposterous to think that the prospects for the UK after leaving the EU may not be as catastrophic, and it may be all right in the end, although with the caveat that it is still early days. The full impact of actually leaving the EU is yet to be fully realised.

However, with respect to some of the flashes of hope stated above, the UK has to believe that the storm will pass and that there's a bright day ahead.

The final chapter of this book is by no means conclusive. We are inching closer to the end game, even though the pre-deal process is currently stalled. Another UK Prime Minister has become a casualty of Brexit, just as the rear guards on a chess board fall on their swords. Let me take this opportunity to draw similarities between the current impasse and a game of chess. Chess is a strategy game that requires internal decision tree style thinking, and high situational awareness. It is a relevant analogy for Brexit not least because of my fondness for the game, but because of the emphasis on strategy and situational awareness - the perception of environmental elements and events with respect to time or space - is critical to the Brexit negotiation process.

Let us assume that the UK electorate is represented by the 'King' (the most important piece) on a chessboard, and the UK Prime Minister is by the 'Queen' (supposedly the most powerful piece in the game). We may liken the current situation to being in 'check' whilst the UK considers its next move. Will it result in checkmate to the EU? Will it end in a stalemate? Or can the UK come up with a stronger counter move? Conservative MPs have taken some time out to focus on electing a new leader and, thus, a new UK Prime Minister. This may be loosely likened to a 'pawn promotion' in a game of chess, a rule that requires a pawn that reaches its eighth rank 'in the battle to be promoted', and becomes the most powerful piece as part of the same move. This type of manoeuvre has some tactical significance in a chess game (and potentially in our current reality) as a 'pawn promotion', or the threat of it, often influences the result of the endgame. Rhetorically, could the new UK Prime Minister reverse the current situation, causing the EU to retreat and make further concessions?.

The Benefit of Hindsight

So, what have we learned with the benefit of hindsight?

It appears that most industries were not well prepared for the referendum result. The results of the debate about the benefits and disadvantages of Brexit remain inconclusive. Within the scope of this book, it is debatable whether the Financial Services industry could have lobbied more effectively, or done more during the last three years to press its case. According to most financial analysts, this has already been 'priced in', but what exactly does this mean? As a financial term, it simply means that all available information is already reflected in the price; the stock price reflects the market's expectations about the company's future success and earnings. For example, if investors believe that the UK will be relatively less attractive in the future for investments; this is already built into UK prices, such as the UK Sterling exchange rate and stocks. So this is already reflected to some extent; most organisations had made contingency provisions in the event that the UK had left the EU on the original departure date. However, the key question remaining is - how well placed is it now to endure the continued uncertainty?

INSERTS B TO E

Insert B: The Winners and Losers of Brexit

Overall, Brexit will have different sectoral impacts from a short- and long-term perspective. Whilst much is still yet to be determined about the shape of the UK and EU negotiations, politics will be critical in shaping the final outcomes of the agreements and this may in turn impact on the economic and business outcomes.

Below is a summary of some industry experts' views of the perceived losers and winners of Brexit, with the caveat that this may not necessarily be a balanced perspective, especially in the case where it is widely known that the expert is biased towards Leave or Remain.

Brexit Losers	Brexit Winners
• **EU** – 'UK and other low-performing EU economies that the UK's contribution goes towards supporting' could be negatively impacted, according to Nicola Horlick. • **High value manufacturing industry** – "Brexit is bad for services if we lose access to the Single [EU] Market, but could be good for manufacturing. However, Brexit will have a negative impact on high value exports, as the cost of importing many parts required to build the final product which is then exported may lead to a net negative impact, especially if the import is from other EU countries. The net effect of importing different parts before exporting the final product may not be positive and it may become necessary to restructure the entire supply chain," according to Jacob Nell.	• **Competing European cities** – "Dublin, Luxembourg, Amsterdam, Paris, and Frankfurt initially appear to be winners, as some businesses from the UK may be lost to these regions; however, with more challenging labour laws in some of these countries, such as France, this may be limited. Luxembourg is coming out a winner, with several large asset managers transferring assets there. Dublin may see a 5% growth, as it is perhaps the closest to the UK in terms of location, culture, language, and architecture," according to Nicola Horlick. o Some financial institutions have confirmed that staff levels at their Dublin branches are predicted to double compared to their pre-Brexit operating capacity, although few jobs in London are expected to be impacted.

- **London** – "London's significance as a global financial centre may diminish following Brexit, because shrinkage of the financial services industry may negatively ripple through the ecosystem, which will be bad for the UK," according to Nicola Horlick.

- **UK citizens** – "The UK economy may lose out where businesses are planning to cut investments or freeze recruitment. For example, approximately one in five organisations are considering moving their operations abroad. The UK people could be worse off from the loss of opportunity," according to Jacob Nell.

- **UK household income** – "Under most scenarios it appears that the UK would lose full access to the Single Market at a cost to the economy estimated at between 1% and 6% of GDP; this represents a significant loss of real income to households," according to Jacob Nell.

- **UK economy** – "UK could possibly move from being the fifth to the seventh biggest economy in the world, therefore setting the UK economy backwards," according to Nicola Horlick.

- **UK importers** – "The BoE could raise interest rates, leading to negative economic consequences due to increased inflation in the UK because of increased import prices," according to Jacob Nell.

- **New York** – "According to James Gorman [CEO of Morgan Stanley] – one of the winners from Brexit could be New York [NY], rather than another European financial centre, as some businesses [swaps] may migrate to NY where there is the infrastructure to deal with the business. For some banks, they may move to NY being their main branch rather than having London as a second financial centre. NY may be a significant winner," according to Jacob Nell.

- **UK low-value exporters** – "Lower sterling is positive for exporters, specifically manufacturers where the impact from a sterling depreciation has been positive," according to Jacob Nell.

Insert C: Brexit Impact Table

This table indicates which economic features are expected to be negatively or positively impacted as a result of Brexit.

Feature	Impact	Description	Source
Agriculture and Fisheries	+	Leaving the EU could lead to this industry's increased prosperity.	Brexit – the movie
Automobile Industry	+ / -	The car industry is a good example of an industry that benefitted from the UK being in the EU. The investments from Nissan, Toyota, BMW, Rolls-Royce, and Tata investing in Land Rover and Jaguar has contributed to the UK being the thirteenth-largest car manufacturer. These firms may be negatively affected when the UK leaves the EU due to the EU's tariff of 10% on new cars and 5% on parts. This may make the UK less competitive and unattractive. Although Nissan has indicated it will remain in the UK, it has been suggested that this will incur some cost for the government.	Campbell (2016)
Consumers	-	It is unclear which group of consumers would win when Brexit occurs, other than perhaps industries with tariffs that protect the UK against imports from the EU. In which case consumers may lose.	OECD (2016)
Employment rate	-	According to a report produced by the Institute of Directors, a quarter of directors are planning to freeze recruitment, with one in five considering moving some operations away from the UK.	Renison (2016)

Educational institutions	-	Over half of the world's economic growth since WWII can be attributed to science and technology. A chaotic Brexit may significantly disrupt the UK's education sector.	Galsworthy & Davidson (2016)
FDI	-	15–25% estimate decrease in investor's appetite for UK assets due to uncertainty.	OECD (2016)
Financial services industry	-	Negatively impacted due to potential restricted access to the Single Market and the requirement to set up a base within the EU. The associated restructuring costs and capital inefficiency.	Interview: Nell (2016)
GDP	-	Potential drop in GDP of more than 1% in perpetuity.	Portes (2016)
Healthcare	-	There appears to be a shortage of healthcare workers such as nurses; as a result, the UK has to procure them from Europe and the Far East. According to The King's Fund report, Brexit has major implications for health and social care in England. Across NHS trusts there is currently a shortage of more than 100,000 staff, severely affecting some key groups of essential staff, including nurses, many types of doctors, and care staff. Brexit and immigration policy will have an impact on the ability of the NHS to successfully fill these vacancies. Additionally, the ageing population is putting a strain on the system as people are living longer and Brexit may exacerbate the issue, due to the shortage of NHS staff.	Interview: Horlick (2016) The King's Fund

Manufacturing: High-value manufacturing (aerospace)	-	There were suggestions that there may be a negative impact on complex exports with cross-border supply chains, as imports become more expensive. Therefore, the cost of importing many parts required to build the final product which is then exported may lead to a net negative impact, especially if the import is from other EU countries.	Interview: Nell (2016)
Low-value widgets	+	More straightforward and easy to see that Brexit may have a positive impact due to the weaker sterling and therefore positively impacting low-value exports.	
Public finances (direct effect)	-	The damage to public finances based on NIESR's estimates could be between £20 and £40 billion in 2019.	NIESR (2016)
Public finances (indirect effect)	-	National debt increases, additional debt interest payments, austerity measures leading to spending cuts and tax rises.	Emmerson et al. (2016)
Public services	+	Approximately £8 billion saving from EU net contribution. This reduction in public spending estimated for 2018 onwards is equivalent to 1% reduction in total spending. This lower spending reduces the gap between public spending and receipts, therefore reducing the public sector net borrowing.	Emmerson et al. (2016)
Technology	-	Brexit may create more challenges in the short term, for FinTech businesses that rely on technology and those that currently procure programmers from Eastern Europe and other emerging countries due to the shortage of these skills in the UK.	Interview: Horlick (2016)

		According to an article by Rhiannon Williams (see article for a more detailed analysis) IT and technology experts have expressed concern over the implications of a no-deal on the country's fledgling start-ups. Simon Hansford, chief executive of UK cloud-hosting supplier UKCLOUD, told the Lords EU committee in February 2019, "We have multiple multimillion-pound investment decisions that need to be made, but it depends on capital, certainty, and access to people."	Rhiannon Williams
		Tech for UK says that Brexit is already having an adverse effect on the UK technology sector.	
		However, tech giants including Facebook, Snap, and Google have expanded their teams in the UK in the wake of the UK's exit from the European Union. Sundar Pichai, Google's chief executive, said the company was 'committed to the UK'. Tim Cook, Apple's chief executive, has also declared the UK will be 'just fine' post-Brexit. "The UK and global technology industry is already in the grips of a major skills shortage. Foreign skilled IT workers, whether from the EU, working in the UK, or UK workers in the EU, feel uncertain over their future, causing a large proportion to return home or to work elsewhere. Technology companies are used to facing disruption, and are arguably more agile than most and less affected by new barriers to physical trade," he added.	
		However, funding for UK tech firms by the European Investment Fund (EIF) fell by 91% during 2017 to €61.1 million (£53 million) compared with €708.8 million the previous year. Therefore the net impact appears to be negative thus far.	
Tourism	+	Potential increase in tourism, due to the weaker sterling exchange rate.	Interview: Anon

Insert D: Ecosystem dynamic effects

Nicola Horlick describes her view of the short-term knock-on effect of Brexit as follows:

> *"The UK economy will be impacted, not just from the loss of labour force to competing cities, but also the knock-on effects from reduced consumer expenditure. For example, if a highly paid financial services worker moves to Frankfurt, and they spend big in Frankfurt, it isn't just one job moved to Frankfurt, but potential loss of jobs in the ecosystem dependent on that financial services worker. These could include housekeepers, schools, nurseries, gardeners, supermarkets, and wherever else they spend their money, such as pubs and restaurants. Essentially, in the short run, the UK economy may be negatively impacted by losing consumers who are big spenders and contributing to the economy."*

See below for an illustration of this ecosystem of financial services staff spending and the short-run knock-on impact if they move away from the UK:

Financial services employee ecosystem		
	Schools	"Loss of fees for private schools if financial services staff move to other European cities with their families,"
	Nurseries and childcare providers	"Similar to the situation as with schools, where a number of nursery places are mostly used by working parents, a significant proportion of whom work in the City,"
	Supermarkets	"Loss of revenue for supermarkets that miss out from these big spenders,"
	Automobile	"There's typically a big contribution from annual bonus purchases,"
	City pubs	"Loss of revenue for pubs that may miss out from these big spenders, which has become part of the City culture,"
	Housing market	"The UK housing market may dampen due to the weaker sterling,"
	Gardener / other housekeepers	"Loss of revenue for domestic workers that are primarily or solely employed by those in financial services."

Figure 16: Short-term impacts on the financial services staff ecosystem

Source: Synthesised by author from the interview discussions

Insert E: The UK's potential trade options and estimated net EU contributions

The different UK options present decreasing levels of access to the Single Market relative to the expected net yearly contributions to the EU budget.

Option / likelihood (%)		Features	Net yearly estimated EU contribution	Source
No / Soft Brexit 10%	Remain in EU	• Maintain existing access to the Single Market. • There's limited disruption on existing business models. • Although most of the interviewees assigned a 10% probability to this outcome, this is highly unlikely given the results of the referendum.	Full access to single market £8bn	IFS
Moderate Brexit 30%	Norwegian deal (EEA)	• This model maintains some access to the Single Market, but with a reduced contribution to EU budget. • Although this option allows participation in some EU programmes, Norway has no influence over EU decisions . • Free movement continues.	£3.3bn	IFS
	Swiss deal (EFTA)	• Contributes to regional development, but to a lesser extent than Norway. • Restricted access to EU financial services markets but not services. • Swiss banks have UK branches in order to access the Single Market.	£90m	IFS

UK's options

| Hard Brexit 60% | Brit deal ('BRETA') | • An opportunity to define new bilateral trading agreements with key trading partners.
• The Canadian agreement signed on 31 October 16 (CETA) sets a good precedent.
• Looser arrangements where the UK avoids contributing to the EU budget, but with reduced access to the EU's services markets. | TBD |
| | WTO rules | • No provision for services.
• Limited access to Single Market. | 0

No access to Single Market |

Source: Adapted by author from interviews and various sources

ADDITIONAL RESOURCES: BREXIT JARGON

Term	Definition
Alignment	Keeping rules and regulations in the UK in line with those in the European Union after Brexit, as in 'regulatory alignment'.
Another referendum	Some campaigners – who call their proposal the People's Vote – want to have another referendum on the UK's membership of the EU. It has been suggested the vote could have three options: Theresa May's deal, no-deal, and remain. But some campaigners think there should only be two choices. Opponents of another vote say there is no need for it, as the 2016 referendum made it clear that people wanted to leave the EU.
Article 50	Part of an EU treaty that sets out how member countries can leave, with a two-year timetable for leaving. Article 50 was triggered by Prime Minister Theresa May at the end of March 2017, and means the UK was supposed to leave the EU at the end of March 2019, but presently extended to 31st October 2019. The UK is allowed to stop the Article 50 process completely, but if it wants only to extend it, all the other EU countries must agree.

Backstop plan	Currently, there are no border posts, physical barriers or checks on people or goods crossing the border between Northern Ireland and the Republic of Ireland. The backstop is a measure in the withdrawal agreement designed to ensure that that continues after the UK leaves the EU. It comes into effect only if the deal deciding the future relationship between the UK and EU is not agreed by the end of the transition period. Until the deal on the future relationship is done, the backstop would keep the UK effectively inside the EU's customs union but with Northern Ireland also conforming to some rules of the Single Market. Critics say a different status for Northern Ireland could threaten the existence of the United Kingdom and fear that the backstop could become permanent.
Brexit	Short for Britain exiting the European Union.
Brexit bus	Refers to a bus hired by the Leave campaign in the run-up to the European Union referendum. On its side was a slogan that became one of the most controversial of the campaign and was credited by some with swinging the result: "We send the EU £350m a week. Let's fund our NHS instead. Vote Leave."
Brexit day	The day when the UK is due to leave the European Union.
Brexiteers / Brexiters	Short for those who are in favour of Brexit.
Brexodus	A combination of the words 'Brexit' and 'exodus' to mean the departure of people or companies from the UK because of Brexit.
Brino	Brexit in name only.
Cake and eat it	A phrase used to mean that Britain is trying to retain all the benefits of European Union membership without the obligations, including payments to the EU budget, accepting jurisdiction of the European Court of Justice, and accepting the free movement of people. European negotiators have frequently used 'cake and eat it' to characterise Britain's approach.

Canada model	Canada has a free trade deal with the EU known as the Comprehensive Economic and Trade Agreement (CETA). Under the deal, most imported goods are not taxed, although there are some additional customs checks. There are some limits, or quotas, on the amount of certain food products, like meat and cereals, that can be imported. Services, like banking, are much more restricted. Canada does not contribute to the EU budget and the principle of free movement does not apply, so Canadians are not free to live and work in the EU.
Canada plus	Some people in favour of leaving the EU have campaigned for the Canada plus or *Canada plus plus* model. The UK would like all the benefits of the Canada deal, plus greater access to the EU for its financial institutions, as well as fewer restrictions on food products and an agreement to recognise the same standards on things like food production to avoid the need for border checks. Canada plus 'plus' refers to a free trade accord with the EU, similar to that negotiated with Canada, and including extremely close relations in security, foreign policy and other areas.
Chequers plan	This plan for Brexit was agreed by the Cabinet at the Prime Minister's country residence, Chequers, in July 2018. It proposed tax or tariff-free trade with the EU, whilst leaving the UK free to pursue trade deals outside the EU. Under the plan, the UK would collect tariffs on the EU's behalf for any goods entering the country but destined to be sent on to EU countries. Because EU tariffs had been collected, there would not need to be a separate border between Northern Ireland and the Republic. But the UK would have to follow EU rules – 'the common rule book' – on things like food standards to avoid unnecessary border hold-ups. The plan also proposed ending the free movement of people, giving back the UK control over immigration rules. Former Brexit Secretary David Davis and former Foreign Secretary Boris Johnson both resigned their posts over the Chequers plan, because they believed it meant the UK would still be too closely tied to the EU.
Cherry picking	A phrase used to mean the UK is trying to choose which European Union arrangements it wants to stay associated with and which it wants to fully opt out of. Similar to 'cake and eat it'.
Cliff edge	A term used by critics of Brexit to describe the prospect of the UK leaving the European Union with no deal at all.

Common Agricultural Policy	The EU policy designed to provide financial support to farmers through a system of payments. It was created to make sure that farmers in the EU produced enough food and also had a fair standard of living. Critics say it is wasteful and favours rich landowners and big agri-businesses.
Council of Ministers	A European Union body that represents member states' national governments. It is made up of government ministers from all member states who meet regularly. Together with the European Parliament, the council has the power to make EU laws and decide the budget.
Customs Union	A trade agreement under which two or more countries do not put tariffs (taxes) on goods coming in from other countries in the union. The countries also decide to set the same tariff on goods entering from outside the union. The EU Customs Union includes EU member states and some small non-EU members and forbids members from negotiating trade agreements separately from the EU. Instead trade agreements are negotiated collectively.
DExEU	The Department for Exiting the European Union: the name of the UK government department responsible for managing the UK's departure from the EU.
Disorderly Brexit	Term used by the Bank of England to describe what could happen if the UK were to leave the EU with no deal and very little notice. The bank has warned that food prices could rise and the economy could be tipped into recession as part of what it has called a 'disorderly Brexit'.
Divergence	Allowing rules and regulations to differ between the European Union and the UK after Brexit.
Divorce bill	The money the UK has agreed to pay to the EU under Theresa May's deal. Based on UK's share of EU budgets up to 2020 as well as continuing liabilities such as EU civil servants' pensions. The bill is widely expected to be about £39 billion and will be paid over a number of years, with about half of it during the transition.
EU	European Union: the political and economic union of twenty-eight member states, which the UK is planning to leave.

EU referendum	A national vote held on 23 June 2016 to decide whether the UK should leave or remain in the European Union. It was decided on a simple majority and the Leave campaign won by 52% to 48%.
European Commission	The European Union's civil service. The European Commission has a key role in initiating EU legislation.
European Council	A body of the European Union that makes its most important strategic decisions. Its members are heads of state or government of the twenty-eight EU countries, the European Council president, and the president of the European Commission.
European Court of Justice (ECJ)	The ECJ is the EU's highest legal authority and rules on disputes over European Union treaties and other EU laws. Its decisions are binding on EU institutions and member states.
European Economic Area (EEA)	An area covering the twenty-eight European Union countries, plus Norway, Iceland, and Liechtenstein, which enables those three countries to be part of the EU's single market. They abide by the rules of the EU Single Market and its freedom of movement of people, goods, services, and money. But Norway, Liechtenstein, and Iceland are not part of the EU's Common Agricultural or Fisheries policies and they do not have a common foreign and security policy.
European Free Trade Association (EFTA)	An organisation made up of four countries: Iceland, Liechtenstein, Norway, and Switzerland. They are allowed to trade freely with the Single Market in return for accepting its rules. They're not in the EU Customs Union and can negotiate trade deals with third-party countries such as China.
European Parliament	The directly elected parliamentary institution of the European Union. It has 751 members and is elected by citizens in all twenty-eight European Union member states.
Eurosceptic	Someone who is opposed to the European Union having too much control, because they think it compromises the power of individual countries to make rules and decide their own destiny. Eurosceptics include those who want to return powers from the EU to member states and those who want their country to leave the EU altogether.

Facilitated customs arrangement	A plan for a post-Brexit customs agreement, in which goods destined for the EU would be charged an EU tariff and goods headed to the UK would be charged the UK's own potentially lower tariff. The plan would keep the UK aligned to EU regulations and is designed to resolve the Irish border question whilst allowing Britain to pursue a partially independent trade policy.
Four freedoms	The free movement of goods, capital, services and people in the EU's Single Market.
Free trade agreement	A deal between countries to reduce, but not necessarily eliminate, trade barriers. These barriers include import or export taxes (tariffs), quotas, or licences that limit imports, and differing regulations on things such as safety, hygiene, or labelling. The aim is to increase trade in goods but also services.
Free movement	One of the four freedoms associated with the Single Market is free movement of people. This lets EU citizens travel, live, study, and work in any member country. There can be no discrimination in access to public services and benefits.
Frictionless trade	Trying to do business between the UK and the European Union with the minimum of tariffs, quotas, customs checks, and other obstructions.
Hard border	A border controlled and protected by customs officials, police, or military personnel.
Hard Brexit	A hard Brexit would be one where few of the existing ties between the UK and the EU were retained. The UK would give up membership of the EU's Single Market and its Customs Union, instead setting up its own trade deals and rules. It is a phrase often used by critics of Brexit who think it will harm the UK economy.
Henry VIII powers	Legal provisions for ministers to decide on changes to existing UK law without the normal process of scrutiny in Parliament. The term is named after King Henry VIII's preference for creating laws by royal proclamation rather than through Parliament.
Irish border	The border between Northern Ireland and the Republic of Ireland. After Brexit, it will become the only land border between the UK and the European Union.

Malthouse compromise	The Malthouse compromise is named after the Housing Minister Kit Malthouse. Its supporters are mostly Conservative Leavers and Remainers. The plan proposes two options. Under the first, the Prime Minister would try to renegotiate the backstop plan to replace it with a free trade agreement and an extended transition period until December 2021. The second option would apply if the attempted renegotiation failed. In this scenario, the UK would leave the European Union without a formal withdrawal agreement, but before leaving, the UK would try to negotiate a three-year transition with the EU to prepare for a no-deal outcome. During that time the UK would continue to contribute financially to the EU.
Managed no-deal	Also sometimes called a negotiated no-deal, promoted by some Brexiteers who want to allay fears about what would happen if the UK left the EU without a deal. This proposes a transition period during which time the UK would negotiate a free-trade deal as a third country. The UK could also strike a number of mini deals to avert chaos in sectors of the economy. Critics say a transition or implementation period is a key component of the Withdrawal Agreement, and if rejected the UK would immediately be subject to WTO rules and have to rely on the goodwill of the EU to resolve any problems.
Mandate	The authority to carry out policy. In relation to Brexit it often refers to the referendum result giving a mandate to the government to take Britain out of the European Union.
Max-fac	'Maximum facilitation' – an option favoured by Brexiteers who want a complete break with the EU customs regime and would rely instead on technology to minimise border checks. Declaration and clearance procedures would take place in advance, away from the border, and surveillance would be intelligence-led, rather than old-fashioned random searches. Critics say it would not solve the Irish border question as there would still need to be tariff checks.
Meaningful vote	The government said Parliament would be given a 'meaningful vote' on the withdrawal deal negotiated by Theresa May with the European Union. This initial vote took place on 15 January 2019 and MPs voted by 432 to 202 to reject the deal. Parliament still needs to approve a deal before it can be implemented.

MEP	Member of the European Parliament. There are currently seventy-three UK MEPs, representing twelve electoral regions made up of the nations and regions of the UK. Elections take place every five years.
No deal	A no-deal Brexit would mean the UK leaving the European Union and cutting ties immediately with no agreement at all in place. The UK would follow World Trade Organization rules to trade with the EU and other countries, whilst trying to negotiate free-trade deals. MPs voted 400 to 160 votes against a no-deal exit on 13 March 2019.
Norway model	The UK would remain in the EU Single Market, able to trade freely, but in return it would have to allow free movement of people – which has been a key sticking point for many in the Brexit debate who want to be able to control immigration from the EU. The UK would also have to make a contribution to the EU budget – smaller than it currently makes – and abide by many of the EU's rules.
Passporting	The arrangement under which British and foreign companies with bases in the UK are allowed to sell financial services across the European Union with no regulatory barriers.
Political declaration	Document which sets out proposals for how the UK's long-term future relationship with the EU will work after Brexit. The political declaration is not legally binding but will be worked up into a full agreement during the transition period.
Remoaners	A derogatory term referring to those who complain about Britain leaving the European Union and/or the outcome of the Brexit referendum.
Schengen area	This is reputed to be the largest free travel area in the world. It is made up of twenty-six European states that have abolished passport controls at their mutual borders so people can travel freely. Some European Union member states, including the UK, are not in the Schengen area. Some countries that are not members of the European Union, like Norway and Iceland, are in the Schengen area.

Settled status	This is a new UK scheme due to open to all EU citizens and their families who have been living in the UK for five years under which they can apply for 'settled status', which will allow them to stay in the UK for as long as they wish. Any child born in the UK to a mother with settled status will automatically become a British citizen. Settled status means you can work in the UK, use the NHS, have access to pensions and benefits, and travel in and out of the UK. It is expected that applications will only be rejected from people with serious criminal convictions, or where there are other security concerns.
Single Market	A system that enables goods, services, people, and capital (money) to move between all twenty-eight EU member states, as well as Iceland, Norway, Liechtenstein, and Switzerland. Countries in the Single Market apply many common rules and standards. A UK company can sell its products (goods) in Portugal as easily as it can in Portsmouth, bring back the cash (capital), offer maintenance (services), and despatch a repair team (people).
Soft Brexit	Leaving the European Union but staying as closely aligned to the EU as possible. This could mean keeping the UK in the Single Market or the Customs Union or both. It could involve the free movement of people continuing. EU citizens would retain the right to settle and work in the UK and have access to public services and benefits; UK citizens would retain the same rights in the EU.
Tariff	A tax or duty to be paid on goods being imported or, very occasionally, exported.
Tariff-free trade	Trade without any taxes or duties to pay when goods are imported or exported.
Transition period	If Theresa May's deal was accepted, this period would last twenty-one months from Brexit day. It could be extended by up to two years if both the UK and the EU wanted. The transition is intended to allow time for the UK and EU to agree their future relationship. The UK would have no say in the making of new EU laws during the transition but would have to follow all EU rules, including freedom of movement.

Treaty	An agreement made under international law between countries or international organisations. A treaty is like a contract, both sides agree to abide by certain terms and conditions and if either side breaks the deal, they can be held liable. The Lisbon Treaty is the international agreement that forms the constitutional basis, or the main principles, for the EU.
White Paper	A white paper is a report produced by the government outlining how it is going to approach a particular issue. The government published a white paper on the UK's future relationship with the EU in July 2018 in which it spelled out its proposals for free trade with Europe, new arrangements for financial services, like banking, as well as plans to allow trade to continue to flow between Ireland and Northern Ireland.
Withdrawal agreement	Theresa May has agreed a deal with the EU on the terms of the UK's departure. It does not determine the UK–EU future relationship. It does include how much money the UK must pay to the EU as a settlement, details of the transition period, and citizens' rights. It also covers the 'backstop', which ensures that no hard border exists between Northern Ireland and the Republic of Ireland after Brexit even if there's no deal on the future relationship in place by the end of the transition period.
WTO rules	If countries don't have free-trade agreements, they usually trade with each other under rules set by the World Trade Organization. Each country sets tariffs – or taxes – on goods entering. For example, cars passing from non-EU countries to the EU are charged at 10% of their value. But tariffs on some agricultural products are much higher – dairy averages more than 35%. If the UK chooses to put no tariffs on goods from the EU, it must also have no tariffs on goods from every WTO member.

Source: BBC

REFERENCES

Amlôt, R. (2016) *BREXIT: UK GDP could fall by 2-4 per cent long-term, say London Business School experts* [Online] Available from: https://www. london.edu/news-and-events/news/leave-vote-could-see-gdp-fall-by-2-4-per-cent-long-term#.V5h58LgrK00

Amos, R., (2019), *Barclays to move £166bn to Ireland over 'no-deal' Brexit fears,* [Online] Available from: https://citywire.co.uk/wealth-manager/news/ barclays-to-move-166bn-to-ireland-over-no-deal-brexit-fears/a1196434

Baker, J., Carreras, O., Ebell, M., Hurst, I., Kirby, S., Meaning, J., Piggott, R., and Warren, J., (2016) NIESR, *The Short-Term Economic Impact of Leaving the EU* [Online] Available from: http://www.niesr.ac.uk/sites/default/ files/publications/National%20Institute%20Economic%20Review-2016-Baker-108-20%20(1).pdf

Barker, R., *Richard's Watch* (2016), *Brexit Prophecies* [Online] Available: https://richards-watch.org/prophecies-on-the-uk-leaving-the-eu/

Barnato, K. (2016) *UK may need more stimulus by summer, says Bank of England* [Online] Available from: http://www.cnbc.com/2016/06/30/brexit-uk-may-need-more-monetary-easing-by-summer-says-bank-of-england.html

Barnes, P., (2019) *Brexit: What happens now?* [Online] Available from: https://www.bbc.co.uk/news/uk-politics-46393399

Beale, I. (2016) FT, *London can remain insurance capital after Brexit – Lloyd's chief* [Online] Available from: https://www.ft.com/content/7941bbda-3893-11e6-9a05-82a9b15a8ee7

Begg, I., Mushövel, F., (2016), *The economic impact of Brexit: jobs, growth and the public finances,* [Online] Available from:https://www.lse.ac.uk/ europeanInstitute/LSE-Commission/Hearing-11---The-impact-of-Brexit-on-jobs-and-economic-growth-sumary.pdf

Bloomberg (2016) *FTSE 100 Index* [Online] Available from: https://www. bloomberg.com/quote/UKX:IND

BoE (2016) *Inflation Report, November 2016* [Online] Available from: https:// www.bankofengland.co.uk/inflation-report/2016/november-2016

BoE (2018), *The Term Funding Scheme: design, operation and impact,* [Online] Available from:https://www.bankofengland.co.uk/quarterly-bulletin/2018/2018-q4/the-term-funding-scheme-design-operation-and-impact

Bower, C. (2016) Imperial College Business School, *"Rational cost-benefit analysis" behind Brexit vote says Prof David Miles CBE* [Online] Available from: http://www3.imperial.ac.uk/newsandeventspggrp/imperialcollege/ newssummary/news_17-10-2016-11-57-30

BBC (2016) *2016 EU Referendum results* [Online] Available from: http:// www.bbc.co.uk/news/politics/eu_referendum/results

BBC (2018), *Liam Fox: No deal most likely Brexit outcome for UK,* [Online] Available from:https://www.bbc.co.uk/news/uk-politics-45073294

BBC *(2019), Brexit: Your simple guide to the UK leaving the EU,* [Online] Available from:https://www.bbc.co.uk/news/uk-46318565

BBC (2019) *In full: Theresa May's Brexit delay request to EU's Donald Tusk* [Online] Available from: https://www.bbc.co.uk/news/uk-politics-47641357

BBC (2019) *Brexit: Petition to revoke Article 50 passes 3m signatures* [Online] Available from: https://www.bbc.co.uk/news/uk-politics-47665929

BBC (2019) *MPs reject all Brexit Options* [Online] Available from: https:// www.bbc.co.uk/news/live/uk-politics-parliaments-47696409

BBC (2019) *Brexit votes: What options are MPs voting on?* [Online] Available https://www.bbc.co.uk/news/uk-politics-47704794

BBC (2019) *Brexit: MPs face new vote on withdrawal deal* [Online] Available: https://www.bbc.co.uk/news/uk-politics-47742395

BBC (2019) *Brexit vote: Another defeat ahead for May?* [Online] Available: https://www.bbc.co.uk/news/uk-politics-47742243

BBC (2019) *Brexit: DUP will vote against deal, says Dodds* [Online] Available: https://www.bbc.co.uk/news/uk-northern-ireland-47736913

BBC (2019) *How did my MP vote on Brexit indicative votes?* [Online] Available: https://www.bbc.co.uk/news/uk-politics-47779783

Brexit, *The movie* [Online] Available from: https://www.youtube.com/

watch?v=UTMxfAkxfQ0

British Bankers Association (2016) *BBA Chief Executive Anthony Browne speech BBA International Banking Conference, 20 October 2016* [Online] Available from: https://www.bba.org.uk/wp-content/uploads/2016/10/20161018-international-banking-conference-speech.pdf

Bruce, A. (2016) *Bank of England readies new blast of QE for post-Brexit Britain* [Online] Available from: http://uk.reuters.com/article/us-britain-boe-qe-analysis-idUKKCN0ZT293

Campbell, D. (2018), *UPDATE: UK likely to sign up for EU financial rule changes,* [Online] Available from:https://citywire.co.uk/wealth-manager/news/update-uk-likely-to-sign-up-for-eu-financial-rule-changes/a1137712?section=wealth-manager

Campbell, D. (2018), *Treasury starts prepping City for no deal Brexit,* [Online] Available from: https://citywire.co.uk/wealth-manager/news/treasury-starts-prepping-city-for-no-deal-brexit/a1145685

Campbell, J. (2019), *Brexit: What are the new ideas for the Irish backstop?* [Online] Available from: https://www.bbc.co.uk/news/uk-northern-ireland-47110707

Campbell, P. (2016) *UK car factories face uncertain future after Brexit* [Online] Available from: https://www.ft.com/content/27d7b066-447c-11e6-b22f-79eb4891c97d

CBI Press team (2018), *8 out of 10 businesses say Brexit hits investment as speed of talks outpaced by reality firms face on ground,* [Online] Available from: http://www.cbi.org.uk/news/8-out-of-10-businesses-say-brexit-hits-investment-as-speed-of-talks-outpaced-by-reality-firms-face-on-ground/

Chapman, B. (2019), *UK house price growth grinds to halt as Brexit uncertainty bites,* [Online] Available from: https://www.independent.co.uk/news/business/news/uk-house-prices-latest-property-market-flat-brexit-uncertainty-nationwide-a8755766.html

Chowla, S., Quaglietti, L., and Rachel, L. (2016) *How have world shocks affected the UK economy?* [Online] Available from: (https://www.bankofengland.co.uk/-/media/boe/files/quarterly-bulletin/2014/how-have-world-shocks-affected-the-uk-economy.pdf?la=en&hash=077CB2EC71F558ADC13CEA4E1F6260F9BBEE7F39)

Chu, B. (2016) *Brexit: Everything could still be OK, says small group of economists who supported Leave,* [Online] Available from: https://www.independent.co.uk/news/business/news/brexit-latest-pound-sterling-economy-economist-leave-everything-could-still-be-ok-a7134956.html

Crafts, N. (2016) NIESR event: *The Economics of the UK's EU membership*

[Online] Available from: http://www.niesr.ac.uk/publications/video-highlights-our-economics-uk%E2%80%99s-eu-membership-event#.WEqUeWZXUZw

Crafts, N. (2016) National Institute of Economic and Social Research, *Nick Crafts - the economics of Brexit* [Online] Available from: http://ukandeu.ac.uk/multimedia/short-term-losses-nick-crafts-on-the-economics-of-brexit/

Crafts, N. (2016) National Institute of Economic and Social Research, *Short-term losses - Nick Crafts on the Economics of Brexit* [Online] Available from: https://www.youtube.com/watch?v=zWr8ZkqCDek

Crisp, J (2019) *We will do everything we can to avoid no deal Brexit, says Angela Merkel* [Online] Available: https://www.telegraph.co.uk/politics/2019/04/04/will-do-everything-can-avoid-no-deal-says-angela-merkel/

Department for Exiting the European Union, (2018), *How to prepare if the UK leaves the EU with no deal* [Online] Available from: https://www.gov.uk/government/collections/how-to-prepare-if-the-uk-leaves-the-eu-with-no-deal

De Novellis, M. (2016) *EU Referendum: B-Schools Fear Disastrous Effect Of A Brexit On UK Business Education* [Online] Available from: http://www.businessbecause.com/news/mba-uk/4017/eu-referendum-b-schools-fear-disastrous-effect-of-a-brexit-on-uk-business-education

Dendrinou, V., Seputyte, M., Fouquet, H., and Wishart, I., (2019) *Macron Gets on Everyone's Nerves With Brexit Tough Guy Act* [Online] Available: https://www.bloomberg.com/news/articles/2019-04-11/macron-gets-on-everyone-s-nerves-with-brexit-hard-man-act?utm_campaign=pol&utm_medium=bd&utm_source=applenews

Dhingra, S., Ottaviano, G., Sampson, T., and Van Reenen, J. (2016a) *The consequences of Brexit for UK trade and living standards* [Online] Available from: http://cep.lse.ac.uk/pubs/download/brexit02.pdf

Dhingra, S., Ottaviano, G., Sampson, T., and Van Reenen, J. (2016b) *The impact of Brexit on foreign investment in the UK*, Centre for Economic Performance (CEP), London School of Economics and Political Science (LSE) [Online] Available from: http://cep.lse.ac.uk/pubs/download/brexit03.pdf

Trading Economics (March 2019) *United Kingdom - Economic Indicators* [Online] Available from: http://www.tradingeconomics.com/united-kingdom/indicators

Emmerson, C., Johnson, P., Mitchell, I., and Phillips, D. (2016) *Brexit and the UK's public finances* [Online] Available from: http://www.ifs.org.uk/publications/8296

European Union (2016), *The benefits of CETA* [Online] Available from: http://trade.ec.europa.eu/doclib/docs/2016/july/tradoc_154775.pdf

European Union (2016) *About the EU* [Online] Available from: https://europa.eu/european-union/about-eu/eu-in-brief_en

EY (2016) *Public statements allay concerns about immediate impact of Brexit on Financial Services, but negotiation priorities vary across sectors* [Online] Available from: http://www.ey.com/uk/en/newsroom/news-releases/16-08-22---public-statements-allay-concerns-about-immediate-impact-of-brexit-on-financial-services--but-negotiation-priorities-vary-across-sectors

EY, (2019), *EY Financial Services Brexit Tracker: Heightened uncertainty drives financial services companies to move almost £800 billion of assets to Europe,* [Online] Available from: https://www.ey.com/uk/en/newsroom/news-releases/19-01-07-ey-financial-services-brexit-tracker-heightened-uncertainty-drives-financial-services-companies-to-move-almost-800-billion-pounds-of-assets-to-europe

Farah,Y. (2018), *Brexodus: why fund firms are moving billions out of UK,* [Online] Available from: https://citywire.co.uk/wealth-manager/news/brexodus-why-fund-firms-are-moving-billions-out-of-uk/a1122814

Farah, Y. (2018) *Peter Hargreaves: no deal Brexit is best option* [Online] Available from: https://citywire.co.uk/wealth-manager/news/peter-hargreaves-no-deal-brexit-is-best-option/a1144727?section=wealth-manager

FCA, *Brexit: information for UK firms (2019)* [Online] Available from: https://www.fca.org.uk/brexit; https://www.fca.org.uk/firms/preparing-for-brexit/uk-firms-considerations; https://www.fca.org.uk/firms/preparing-for-brexit

Fetzer, T. (2018) *Austerity swung voters to Brexit – and now they are changing their minds* [Online] Available: https://blogs.lse.ac.uk/brexit/2018/11/19/austerity-swung-voters-to-brexit-and-now-they-are-changing-their-minds/

Full Fact (2016) *EU facts behind the claims: economic costs and benefits* [Online] Available from: https://fullfact.org/europe/economic-costs-and-benefits-eu-membership/

Galsworthy, M., Davidson, R., Scientists for EU (2016) *Brexit is damaging UK science already. Here is a plan to fix it* [Online] Available from http://blogs.lse.ac.uk/brexit/2016/09/29/brexit-is-damaging-uk-science-already-here-is-a-plan-to-fix-it/

Gandrud, C. (2016) *The return of the British Disease? The post-Brexit credible commitment conundrum* [Online] Available from: http://blogs.lse.ac.uk/politicsandpolicy/the-return-of-the-british-disease/

Garrett, G. (2016) *Brexit Aftershocks Are Creating Greater Uncertainty*

[Online] Available from: https://www.linkedin.com/pulse/brexit-aftershocks-creating-greater-uncertainty-geoffrey-garrett?trk=eml-b2_content_ecosystem_digest-hero-14-null&midToken=AQHx_EAU0U37oA&fromEmail=fromEmail&ut=3jBU9AKr60gnk1

Henley, J., Rankin, J., and Oltermann, P. (2016) *European leaders rule out informal Brexit talks before article 50 is triggered* [Online] Available from: http://www.theguardian.com/politics/2016/jun/27/europe-leaders-crunch-talks-brexit-fallout

Hill, S. (2016) *Post-Brexit: EU Still a Superpower* [Online] Available from: http://www.theglobalist.com/post-brexit-eu-still-a-superpower/

Hills, J. (2016) *Leave vote likely to trigger 'significant sell-off in Sterling'* [Online] Available from: http://www.itv.com/news/2016-06-21/leave-vote-likely-to-trigger-significant-sell-off-in-sterling/

Hill, P., Korczak, A., and Korczak, P. (2019) *How Brexit has hit the value of UK firms* [Online] Available from https://blogs.lse.ac.uk/brexit/2019/03/04/how-brexit-has-hit-the-value-of-uk-firms/

Hill, P., Korczak, A., and Korczak, P. (2019), *Political uncertainty exposure of individual companies: The case of the Brexit referendum,* [Online] Available from: https://www.sciencedirect.com/science/article/pii/S0378426618302814?dgcid=author

HM Treasury (2016) *Forecasts for the UK economy: October 2016* [Online] Available from: https://www.gov.uk/government/statistics/forecasts-for-the-uk-economy-october-2016

Hoggett Bowers (2016) *Brexit – The Great Conundrum* [Online] Available from: http://www.hoggett-bowers.com/Other_Events_and_Insights/Brexit_The_Great_Conundrum.aspx

Horlick, N. (2016) *Brexit would undo decades' worth of progress* [Online] Available from: http://www.prospectmagazine.co.uk/politics/brexit-eu-referendum-economic-progress

Hughes, M. (2016) Office of National Statistics, *GDP growth forecasts* [Online] Available from: http://www.ons.gov.uk/economy/governmentpublicsectorandtaxes/researchanddevelopmentexpenditure/bulletins/ukgrossdomesticexpenditureonresearchanddevelopment/2015-03-20

Hussain,N.Z., Nadkar, T., (2018) *DFS Furniture expects Brexit to hit consumer demand,* [Online] Available from: https://uk.reuters.com/article/uk-dfs-furn-results/dfs-furniture-profit-slammed-by-heat-wave-weak-demand-idUKKCN1ME0L8

Inman, P., Collinson, P., Osborne, H., and Butler, S. (2016) *Shares down, jobs down, prices up? Business comes to terms with Brexit* [Online] Available from: http://www.theguardian.com/politics/2016/jun/25/business-comes-to-terms-brexit-shares-jobs-prices

Inman, P., (2019), *One in three UK firms plan for Brexit relocation, IoD says,* [Online] Available from: https://www.theguardian.com/politics/2019/feb/01/one-three-uk-firms-activate-plans-move-operations-abroad-no-deal-brexit-iod-survey

Institute of Directors (2016) *The IoD's Brexit briefing pack* [Online] Available from: https://www.iod.com/news-campaigns/news/articles/The-IoDs-Brexit-briefing-pack

Institute of Directors (2019), *Brexit – ten things directors should consider next*, [Online] Available from: https://www.iod.com/services/information-and-advice/resources-and-factsheets/details/Brexit-ten-things-directors-should-consider-next

Institute of Directors (2019), *'Settled Status' – What will happen to EU Nationals living and working in the UK as a result of Brexit* [Online] Available from: https://www.iod.com/news/navigating-brexit-for-business/articles/settled-status--what-will-happen-to-eu-nationals-living-and-working-in-the-uk-as-a-result-of-brexit-wbb

Interviews:

Horlick, N. Interviewed by: Ani, P. (27 October 2016)

Nell, J. Interviewed by: Ani, P. (24 October 2016)

Spink, H. Interviewed by: Ani, P. (8 November 2016)

Ward, R. Interviewed by: Ani, P. (8 November 2016)

Investment week (2019), *Oeics vs Sicavs* , [Online] Available from: https://www.investmentweek.co.uk/investment-week/analysis/1382331/oeics-vs-sicavs

Jacobides, M. (2016) *Brexit thrusts investors into limbo* [Online] Available from: http://edition.cnn.com/videos/tv/2016/06/26/exp-brexit-thrusts-economy-into-limbo.cnn

James, S. (2016) *The UK's financial services sector is divided over the referendum vote* [Online] Available: https://blogs.lse.ac.uk/brexit/2016/03/22/the-uks-financial-services-sector-is-divided-over-the-referendum-vote/

Jenkins, P., Agnew, H. (2016) *What the City stands to lose and gain from Brexit – Sectors such as foreign exchange trading have boomed during EU years* [Online] Available from: https://www.ft.com/content/807750a4-d984-11e5-98fd-06d75973fe09

Jenkins, P. (2016) Financial Times, *What would Brexit mean for the City of*

London? [Online] Available from: https://www.ft.com/content/f44e8a6e-2f2a-11e6-bf8d-26294ad519fc

Johnson, P. (2016*) We are in uncharted waters without a compass* [Online] Available from: http://www.ifs.org.uk/publications/8337

Khan, M. (2016), *What would Brexit mean for the City of London?* [Online] Available from: http://www.telegraph.co.uk/business/2016/05/18/what-will-brexit-mean-for-the-city-of-london/

Kierzenkowski, R., Pain, N., Rusticelli, E., Zwart, S. (2016) OECD, *The Economic Consequences of Brexit: A Taxing Decision* [Online] Available from: https://www.oecd.org/eco/The-Economic-consequences-of-Brexit-27-april-2016.pdf

Kollewe, J. (2016) *Lloyd's considers opening EU subsidiary to be ready for Brexit* [Online] Available from: https://www.theguardian.com/business/2016/sep/22/brexit-vote-imajor-lloyds-insurance-markets-profits-rise

Lamont, N. (2016) National Institute of Economic and Social Research, *There's life outside the EU – Lord Norman Lamont on the Economics of Brexit* [Online] Available from: https://www.youtube.com/watch?v=7Tp0GZOOCvU&list=PL6X79_NZm62heZ6_z2BcorlWd6IVaP5-P

Lee, A. (2016) *Strategic Problem Solving* [Lecture] Imperial College Business School

London Business School (2016) *BREXIT: UK GDP could fall by 2-4 per cent long-term, say London Business School experts,* [Online] Available from: https://www.london.edu/news-and-events/news/leave-vote-could-see-gdp-fall-by-2-4-per-cent-long-term#.V5h58LgrK00

London Stock Exchange (2016) *FTSE100 Index* [Online] Available from: http://www.londonstockexchange.com/exchange/prices-and-markets/stocks/indices/summary/summary-indices-chart.html?index=UKX

Monaghan, A. (2019) *Pound rises against euro after Brexit deadline extension* [Online] Available from: https://www.theguardian.com/business/live/2019/mar/22/pound-strengthens-on-brexit-extension-business-live?page=with:block-5c948b20e4b0480f6c023b26#block-5c948b20e4b0480f6c023b26

Massey, F. (2016) Office of National Statistics, *Assessment of the UK post-referendum economy: September 2016 (Latest release)* [Online] Available from: http://www.ons.gov.uk/search?q=brexit

Miles, D., Scott, A., and Breedon F. (2012) *Macroeconomics – Understanding the Global Economy,* 3rd edition, Wiley.

McKenna, H., and Baird, B., (2019), *The King's Fund – Brexit: the implications for health and social care,* [Online] Available from: https://www.kingsfund.org.uk/publications/articles/brexit-implications-health-social-care

Miles, D., Perkmann, M., Walker, D., and Petroff, A. (2016) *How will Brexit impact Business as we know it?* https://wwwf.imperial.ac.uk/business-school/how-will-brexit-impact-business-as-we-know-it/

Mineo, L. (2016) *After Brexit, a changed future* [Online] Available from: http://news.harvard.edu/gazette/story/2016/06/after-brexit-a-changed-future/?utm_source=linkedin&utm_medium=social&utm_campaign=hu-linkedinuniversity-general

Moody, A. (2016) China Daily Europe, *Brexit strategy* [Online] Available from:http://europe.chinadaily.com.cn/epaper/2016-06/17/content_25741283.htm

Nagraj, A. (2016) *Brexit: How will it impact the GCC?* [Online] Available from: http://gulfbusiness.com/brexit-how-will-it-impact-the-gcc/#.V5h-H7grK00

Nell, J., Baker, M., Morgan Stanley Research (2016) *EU Exit: Resisting Recession* [Published article]

Nell, J., Goodhart, C., Baker, M., Secker, G., Manners, C., Simpson, F., Ashworth, N. J., Heese, A., Gysens, B., Morgan Stanley Research (2016), *Will The UK Reset Fiscal Policy?* [Published article 29 September 2016]

O'Carroll, L., *(2019), Brexit: Netherlands talking to 250 firms about leaving UK,* [Online] Available from: https://www.theguardian.com/politics/2019/feb/09/brexit-uk-companies-discuss-moving-to-netherlands

OECD (2016) *OECD Economic Surveys: European Union 2016*, OECD Publishing, Paris, https://www.oecd.org/eco/surveys/european-union-2016-overview.pdf

Office of National Statistics, (2018), *GDP monthly estimate, UK: December 2018,* [Online] Available from: https://www.ons.gov.uk/economy/grossdomesticproductgdp/bulletins/gdpmonthlyestimateuk/december2018

Office of National Statistics, *Gross Domestic Product (GDP) QMI*(2016 – 2018) [Online] Available from: http://www.ons.gov.uk/economy/grossdomesticproductgdp/qmis/grossdomesticproductgdpqmi

Osborne, G., Stern, N., Flanders, S., Darling, A., and Cable, V. (2016) *What Next for Growth in the UK?* http://www.lse.ac.uk/publicEvents/events/2016/11/20161102t1830vLSE.aspx. [Lecture] London School of Economics

Oxford Economics,(2016), *Assessing the economic implications of Brexit,* [Online] Available from: https://www.oxfordeconomics.com/recent-releases/assessing-the-economic-implications-of-brexit

Pitas, C., (2019), *UK new car sales slump ahead of Brexit 'existential threat'*, [Online] Available from: https://uk.reuters.com/article/uk-britain-economy-autos-idUKKCN1P10AX

Portes, R. (2016), *Worst of City Brexit losses still to come, expert warns* [Online] Available from: https://www.london.edu/news-and-events/news/worst-of-city-brexit-losses-still-to-come-expert-warns-1030#. WAYuVeArK00

PricewaterhouseCoopers (PwC) (2016), *Leaving the EU: Implications for the UK economy* [Online] Available from: http://www.pwc.co.uk/economic-services/assets/leaving-the-eu-implications-for-the-uk-economy.pdf Report commissioned by The Confederation of British Industry (CBI).

Quinn, J. (2016) *BBA chief warns some bankers could leave London if City does not get strong Brexit deal* [Online] Available from: http://www.telegraph.co.uk/business/2016/10/23/bba-chief-warns-some-bankers-could-leave-london-if-city-does-not/

Renison, A. (2015) *The UK's relationship with the European Union* [Online] Available from: https://www.iod.com/news-campaigns/news/articles/The-UKs-relationship-with-the-European-Union

Renison, A. (2016) Institute of Directors, *Brexit – what it means for your business* [Online] Available from: http://www.director.co.uk/brexit-what-it-means-for-your-business-0607/

Rogers, I., (2019) *9 Lessons in Brexit*, Short Books

Sampson, T., Dhingra, S., , Ottaviano, G., and Van Reenen, J. (2016) *Economists for Brexit: A Critique*, [Online] Available from: http://cep.lse.ac.uk/pubs/download/brexit06.pdf

Sandhu, S. (2019) *What is no-deal Brexit? The consequences of the UK leaving the EU without a deal* [Online] Available from: https://inews.co.uk/news/brexit/no-deal-brexit-what-meaning-uk-leave-uk-consequences/

Sants, H., Hunt, P., Austen, M., Kelly, D. and Naylor, L. (2016) Oliver Wyman, *The Impact of the UK's exit from the EU on the UK-based Financial Services sector* http://www.oliverwyman.com/content/dam/oliver-wyman/global/en/2016/oct/Brexit_POV.PDF

Saunders, M., Lewis, P., Thornhill, A. (2012) *Research Methods for Business Students*, Financial Times/ Prentice Hall; 6th edition

Serhan, Y. (2019) *The Rare Businesses That Can't Wait for Brexit* [Online] Available: https://www.theatlantic.com/international/archive/2019/04/rare-business-cant-wait-brexit/586213/

Smith, D. (2016) *Britain after Brexit: will something continue to turn up?* http://blogs.lse.ac.uk/brexit/event/britain-after-brexit-will-something-continue-to-turn-up/

Stone, J. (2019) *Brexit: EU leaders decide UK's fate behind closed doors as Theresa May secures Article 50 extension* [Online] Available from: https://www.independent.co.uk/news/uk/politics/brexit-article-50-extension-delay-theresa-may-eu-latest-a8834456.html

The Data Team (2016) The Economist, *Britain votes to leave the EU* [Online] Available from http://www.economist.com/blogs/graphicdetail/2016/06/daily-chart-17

The CityUk (2016) *Brexit and The Industry* [Online] Available from: https://www.thecityuk.com/research/brexit-and-uk-based-financial-and-related-professional-services/

The Economist (2018), *The truth about a no-deal Brexit*, [Online], Available from: https://www.economist.com/leaders/2018/11/24/the-truth-about-a-no-deal-brexit

Trading economics (2016) *UK GDP* [Online] Available from: http://www.tradingeconomics.com/united-kingdom/gdp

Treanor, J. (2016) *'Significant' risk to UK firms if passporting rights lost after Brexit* [Online] Available from: https://www.theguardian.com/politics/2016/sep/20/passporting-rights-brexit-uk-firms-fca-eu

UK Parliament (2016) *Brexit – Impact across policy areas* [Online] Available from http://researchbriefings.parliament.uk/ResearchBriefing/Summary/CBP-7213#fullreport

Ullah, S. (2016) *How important is UK financial services trade with the EU?* [Online] Available from: https://colresearch.typepad.com/colresearch/2016/08/how-important-is-uk-financial-services-trade-to-the-eu.html

Varoufakis, Y., Jones, O., Prentoulis, M., Womack, A., and Sarkar, A. (2016) *Brexit Britain: What went wrong and what next?* http://blogs.lse.ac.uk/brexit/event/brexit-britain-what-went-wrong-and-what-next/ [Lecture] London School of Economics

Varoufakis, Y. (2016) *Draft proposal regarding DiEM25's Brexit stance*, PAPER

Véron, N. (2016), *The City of London will decline – and we will all be the poorer for it* [Online] Available from: http://blogs.lse.ac.uk/brexit/2016/09/15/the-city-of-london-will-decline-and-we-will-all-be-the-poorer-for-it/

Warren, T., James, S., and Kassim, H. (2019) *What explains the City of London's ineffectiveness at shaping the Brexit negotiations?* [Online]

Available: https://blogs.lse.ac.uk/brexit/2019/04/08/how-can-we-explain-the-city-of-londons-ineffectiveness-at-shaping-the-brexit-negotiations/

Wasserman, N. (2008) *The Founder's Dilemma* [Online] Available from https://hbr.org/2008/02/the-founders-dilemma

Wells, D. (2018) *What effect will Brexit have on the UK's tech industry?* [Online] Available from: https://www.talentinternational.com/news-uk-what-effect-will-brexit-have-on-the-uks-tech-industry/

White, S., Amato, N., and Vollmer, S. (2016) *Businesses consider the effects of UK decision to leave the EU* [Online] Available from: http://www.cgma.org/Magazine/News/Pages/effects-of-brexit-201614728.aspx?TestCookiesEnabled=redirect

Wikipedia (2016) *European Union* [Online] Available from: https://en.wikipedia.org/wiki/European_Union

Wikipedia (2016) *Brexit* [Online] Available from: https://en.wikipedia.org/wiki/Brexit

Williams, R. (2018) *What a no-deal Brexit could mean for the UK's technology sector* [Online] Available from: https://inews.co.uk/news/technology/no-deal-brexit-uk-technology-industry-sector/

Wilson, H. (2018) *Treasury gets 'no-deal' Brexit plans ready for City* [Online] Available from: https://www.thetimes.co.uk/edition/business/treasury-gets-no-deal-brexit-plans-ready-for-city-002rsq583

World Trade Organization (2016) *Principles of the trading system* [Online] Available from: https://www.wto.org/english/thewto_e/whatis_e/tif_e/fact2_e.htm

Wright, O., and Jones, C. (2019) *World's top wealth fund puts billions into Britain* [Online] Available from: https://www.thetimes.co.uk/article/world-s-top-wealth-fund-puts-billions-into-britain-qswjw8637